OVERLOOK ILLUSTRATED LIVES:

VLADIMIR NABOKOV

Jane Grayson is a lecturer in Russian at the School of
Slavonic and East European Studies, University College
London, and a leading specialist on Nabokov. Her most
recent publication is *Nabokov s World*, two volumes of
essays co-edited with Arnold McMillin and Priscilla
Meyer.

Vladimir Nabokov

Jane Grayson

OVERLOOK PRESS
WOODSTOCK & NEW YORK

First published in the United States in 2002 by
The Overlook Press, Peter Mayer Publishers, Inc.
Woodstock & New York

WOODSTOCK:
One Overlook Drive
Woodstock, NY 12498
www.overlookpress.com
[For individual orders, bulk and special sales, contact our Woodstock office]

NEW YORK:
141 Wooster Street
New York, NY 10012

Published by arrangement with Penguin Books Ltd.

A CIP record for this book is available from the Library of Congress

Printed and bound in Great Britain by The Bath Press

9 8 7 6 5 4 3 2 1
ISBN 1-58567-263-7

frontispiece *Nabokov, Paris, 1939*

For my best reader

Contents

Acknowledgements

All Nabokovians, myself included, owe a great deal to previous scholars and biographers, and, for knowledge of Nabokov's life, to Andrew Field, and Brian Boyd in particular. Yet the humbling realization that comes with writing even such a short biography as this, is just how many facts there are to the telling of a man's life, and just how much there is to get wrong. Despite my best efforts no doubt mistakes remain, but it is not for want of generous and patient help from colleagues all over the world. I thank them all, and I thank Dmitri Nabokov most especially: Gennady Barabtarlo, Evgeny Belodubrovsky, Brian Boyd, Nathalie Clark, Sigrun Frank-Golpon, Derek Glass, Igor Golomshtock, Christopher, Ann and Jon Grayson, Elena Itkina, Larissa Kashuk, Liubov Klimenko, Irina Korasik, Don Barton Johnson, Michael Juliar, Yuri Leving, Priscilla Meyer, Rachel Morley, Eugeny Pasternak, Daniela Rippl, Stacy Schiff, Aleksandr Semochkin, Oxana Shkolnik, Iuliya Solonovich, John Sullivan, Lidia Tanguy, Tatiana Turtanova, Grigory Utgof, Olga Voronina, John Wieczorek, Jackie Wullshlager, Dieter Zimmer, Zinovy Zinik.

My thanks also to: the British Newspaper Library at Colindale; the Nabokov Archive, Montreux; the Nabokov Museum, St Petersburg; the Nabokov Museum at Rozhdestveno; the Russian Historical Museum, Moscow; the Russian Museum, St Petersburg; the Tretyakov Gallery, Moscow; and to my MA Nabokov class of 1999–2000.

Finally, my gratitude and admiration for the skill of the editorial and design staff at Penguin in making light work of shoehorning a heavily illuminated manuscript into a pocketable tome.

VLADIMIR NABOKOV

Border Crossings: 1899–1977

> Lolita *is famous not I. I am an obscure, doubly obscure, novel-*
> *ist with an unpronounceable name.*
>
> (*Strong Opinions*, Interview 1966)

Yes, Nabokov is famous for *Lolita*. But not only *Lolita* – for *Pnin*, for *Pale Fire* and *Ada*, for *The Defense*, *Despair*, *The Gift* and much much more. And the 'double obscurity' of which he spoke in the mid-1960s has, since the raising of the Iron Curtain, turned into fame on both sides of the footlights for this Anglo-Russian author.

It is a rare achievement to make a successful career as a writer in two languages. And if the thrusting ambition and the arrogance of some of his public statements seem calculated to rebuff sympathy, this is a very real case of triumph over adversity, turning losses into gains, constraints into freedoms. Nabokov's first irretrievable loss was his homeland, Russia. His was a privileged aristocratic Russian childhood, with town and country houses, French and English governesses, regular summer visits to Europe. In 1916 when he was just seventeen he inherited a mansion, an estate and a fortune from his uncle. But with the 1917 Revolution it was goodbye to all that. His father's high political profile (he was a prominent member of the liberal Constitutional Democratic Party) made flight the only option for the family. So when Nabokov left Russia in 1919 it was in the knowledge that he would very probably never be going back. He never did. The sense of finality was underscored three years later in 1922 when his father was killed as he was chairing a political meeting in Berlin, caught by a bullet intended for the guest speaker, Pavel Milyukov.

Nabokov spent the years from 1919 to 1940 in Western Europe where, as Vladimir Sirin, he became a Russian writer, publishing in the émigré press in the two main centres of the Russian emigration, Berlin and Paris.

The move to America was again not a freely chosen one, but made in response to pressure of circumstances. Towards the end of the 1930s the future for émigré writers writing in Russian was, to say the least, bleak. Publishing houses were closing down and readership was dwindling. Nabokov was, moreover, married to a Jew. The departure for America just anticipated the Nazi advance on Paris. These were the necessities that compelled him to switch languages and start over again.

It was his fluency in English that gave Nabokov the key to a new career, but the difficulties were, as can well be imagined, much more than purely linguistic. They involved the acquisition of a whole new literary identity, writing for an entirely different readership in an entirely different cultural environment.

How did he cope and retain a sense of self? How did he decide what to jettison and what to salvage? What was he to do with the Russian novels and all the short stories, not to mention the poetry and the plays, that had made his name as the leading writer of the younger generation of Russian émigrés? Was he simply to write them off, or break them up and reuse some of their parts? Or, the ideal but seemingly impossible solution, try to carry them across somehow entire? And what was he to do with his cultural heritage, with the writers and poets so familiar and dear to him and his fellow Russians, yet many of whom were virtually unknown to American readers? Was he simply to throw them overboard as excess baggage, as the iconoclastic Futurists had threatened to do at the start of the century?

The first answer he found was to build a pontoon bridge out of autobiography and self-translation. By the late 1930s before he left Europe he had already made English translations of two of his Russian novels (*Despair* and *Laughter in the Dark*) and preliminary

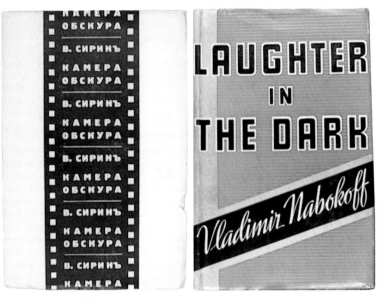

sketches, with revealing titles such as *It is Me*, of his autobiography, *Speak, Memory*. The processes of self-translation and autobiography are linked, and he found both extraordinarily liberating. They involved him stepping outside himself and passing, Alice-like, through the looking-glass. From this position beyond the mirror he could look back to a previous version of self and forward to a self as he envisaged it perceived by other eyes, other readers. Here he experienced not loss or constraint but exhilarating freedom, and could do what it might be imagined only the ghosts of the dead can do: rewind the tape, fast forward, pause and replay. Only ghosts and artists.

Later, but only in the 1960s after the success of *Lolita*, and after his return to Europe, he began systematically transferring the bulk of his Russian work into English. He also returned to autobiography, preparing a revised version, which he entitled *Speak, Memory:*

An Autobiography Revisited, to stand alongside a Russian version he had made in 1954. At this point the severed halves of Nabokov's world at last began to knit together and the Nabokov project could be realized: a body of work in Russian matched by an equivalent body of work in English, with translation and autobiography no longer serving as emotional props, but as the control centre, managing shifts of language and cultural reference, and teasing, challenging the reader to see the connections, the interlocking unity. *Speak, Memory* is a magic carpet made up of an intricate weave of thematic threads, which transport author and reader effortlessly through time and space. The eleven-year-old Nabokov can plunge, butterfly net in hand, into marshland outside St Petersburg and emerge thirty-five years later in the 1940s, still clutching his net, in the Colorado Rockies. Looking back on his life the older Nabokov takes pleasure in noting the symmetrical pattern of his Russian, European and American periods of residence, seeing the nigh-on twenty-year arcs formed by each as a freely evolving upward spiral, escaping the vicious circle of conventional space-time.

This is both psychologically understandable and artistically satisfying. All writers, after all, are weavers of patterns, and Nabokov is a master of the art. Yet appreciation of the design will not prevent a reader asking, 'How much is true?'

In preparing the English versions of some of his Russian novels Nabokov does in fact perform some fairly extensive cosmetic surgery to bring them in line with his later English production. His second Russian novel, *King, Queen, Knave*, published 1928, was so thoroughly revamped in its 1968 translation as to render the garish paperback trumpeting it as 'by the author of *Lolita* and *Ada*' not such a glaring anachronism after all.

In the autobiography, too, he makes good use of the airbrush and masking tape. An experienced reader of Nabokov's fiction will know that the puzzles they contain are all there to be solved. But this does not apply to the telling of the life. Despite the invitation to play the game of 'Find What the Sailor Has Hidden' at the end of *Speak,*

Dust jacket of King, Queen, Knave *by Vladimir Nabokov, translated from the Russian by Dmitri Nabokov with the author. First American paperback edition (Greenwich, CT: Fawcett Crest, 1969).*

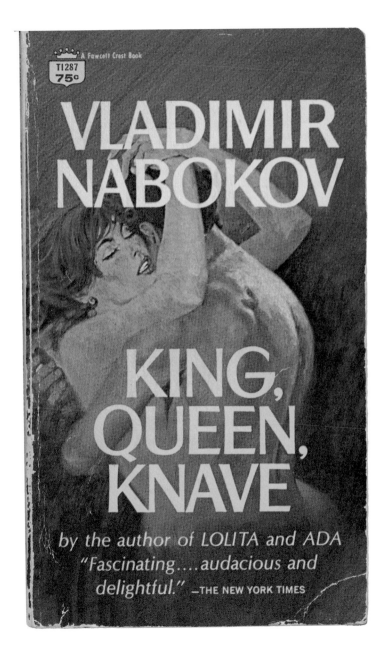

A Fawcett Crest Book

T1287
75c

VLADIMIR NABOKOV

KING, QUEEN, KNAVE

by the author of LOLITA and ADA
"Fascinating....audacious and
delightful." —THE NEW YORK TIMES

Memory, with its reference to patterns that once seen cannot be unseen, and its implied assurance that the answers are always there to be found if a reader only knows where to look, there *are* silences and gaps in Nabokov's autobiographical account, doors – on to marital infidelity, for instance – he prefers to keep firmly shut. What is the curious reader to do? The watchword of Nabokov's art is control. His image of the freely moving rainbow-coloured spiral is, on closer inspection, not freely moving at all: it is encased in glass. It is a child's marble: 'A colored spiral in a small ball of glass, this is how I see my own life.'

The famous author of later years did not hide himself away like a Garbo in his fortress Montreux Palace Hotel, but the Nabokov game was to be played to his rules. He gave interviews, but these interviews had to be carefully scripted, with all questions submitted beforehand in writing. His mastery of disguise and self-parody could hoodwink the unwary. His first biographer, Andrew Field, recorded him saying with a straight face when speaking of his ancestry: 'Yes, sometimes I feel the blood of Peter the Great in me.' The acerbity and *hauteur* were enough to make many a hardy spirit quail.

Question: What is your position in the world of letters?
Answer: Jolly good view from up here.

(*Strong Opinions*, Interview 1971)

The conventions of the Nabokov game have it that the hidden treasure lies within his enchanted garden, not without, and when the inquisitive, sceptical or unsporting ignore the directive and go digging for dark secrets beyond its walls, as often as not they find nothing but dust, and are banished from the kingdom as traitors. Moreover, within the garden stands a mirror, which can draw the reader into its depths. Just as Nabokov issued a health warning to readers of Gogol: 'a man's eyes may become gogolized', so readers of Nabokov must be cautioned lest they return from

Nabokov in 1929 at work on Zashchita Luzhina (The Defense) in a hotel at Le Boulou, east Pyrenees: 'In my twenties and early thirties, I used to write, dipping pen in ink and using a new nib every other day ...' (Strong Opinions, Interview 1967)

behind the mirror speaking only 'nabokovese'. Yet all the spells and enthralment have not stopped plain readers asking plain questions. Was he changed by success? Why all the smokescreens and mystification? Is self-aware snobbery not still snobbery? What is a fastidious Old-World gentleman doing publishing in *Playboy*? Why the predilection for unsavoury subjects: paedophilia and incest, the love of a dwarf or a siamese twin?

It all comes down to a question of balance. The borders that Nabokov crosses in his writing are not simply geographical and linguistic. He is continually, both thematically and stylistically, exploring borderlines – between reality and fantasy, sense and nonsense, sanity and madness, love and lust, the cosmic and the comic. In his very best writing he toes this fine line, the tightrope of parody he has his writer-hero Fyodor speak of in his last Russian novel, *The Gift*. However, does he unfailingly succeed? Does he not, in his last works, it has been suggested, overbalance, cross over into reflexiveness and self-parody?

But before the high-wire act of the art came the

opposite *Nabokov writing at his lectern in Montreux, Switzerland, 1966:* 'I generally start the day at a lovely old-fashioned lectern I have in my study. Later on, when I feel gravity nibbling at my calves, I settle down in a comfortable armchair alongside an ordinary writing desk; and finally, when gravity begins climbing up my spine, I lie down on a couch in a corner of my small study. It is a pleasant solar routine.' *(Strong Opinions, Interview 1964)*

below *Nabokov composing* Lolita *'on the road' in America in the late 1940s and early 1950s – a reconstruction for* Life *magazine, 1958:* 'In the late thirties [. . .] I switched to another, physically more practical, method – that of writing with an eraser-capped pencil on index cards.' *(Strong Opinions, Interview 1967)*

first literal crossing of borders – leaving Russia. It was in Russia that he stored up not just knowledge and memories, but also a way of seeing the world that was to sustain him in his European exile and ultimately enable him to unlock a new world in America. As a young child regular destinations for walks with his nanny and governess were the Aleksandrovsky Gardens behind the family house, by the Admiralty. There stands a charming statue with a saddled camel kneeling in front, its back shiny with the rubbing of generations of young children who have clambered and still clamber upon it. It commemorates the Central Asian naturalist-explorer Colonel Przhevalsky. Here is a real-life model for the fictional character of Fyodor's father in *The Gift* – the famous naturalist Count Konstantin Godunov-Cherdyntsev. Here is an emblem of Nabokov the writer, crossing the borders into art.

Monument to Colonel Nikolai M. Przhevalsky, erected in the 1890s in the Aleksandrovsky (now Admiralty) Gardens, St Petersburg. The inscription reads: 'To Przhevalsky (1839–1888) first naturalist explorer of Central Asia.'

Russia: 1899–1919

I was a perfectly normal trilingual child in a family with a large library. (*Strong Opinions*, Interview 1964)

I don't think in any language. I think in images. (*Strong Opinions*, Interview 1962)

There were some 5,000 books in Nabokov's father's library. There were the law books, of course, for V. D. Nabokov was a lawyer by training, and the books on sociology, politics and economics, which reflected his father's other professional interests, but the second largest section was literature: fiction, poetry and drama in Russian, English and French, as well as German and other languages. Here between the ages of ten and fifteen Nabokov read more prose and poetry than in any other five-year period of his life, and he remembered later the lasting pleasure he found in H. G. Wells and Edgar

Ex libris Vladimir Dmitrievich Nabokov: 'When the Soviet Revolution made it imperative for us to leave St Petersburg, that library disintegrated, but queer little remnants of it kept cropping up abroad. Some twelve years later, in Berlin, I picked up from a bookstall one such waif, bearing my father's *ex libris*. Very fittingly, it turned out to be *The War of the Worlds* by Wells.' *(Speak, Memory, Chapter 9)*

Allan Poe, Browning and Keats, Flaubert, Verlaine and Rimbaud, Chekhov, Tolstoy and Aleksandr Blok. The library was a long panelled room situated at the far end of the ground floor of the three-storey St Petersburg mansion. This was 47 Bolshaya Morskaya, a smart address, just a few minutes' walk from Mariinskaya Square and St Isaac's Cathedral, and beyond that Palace Square and the government buildings where Nabokov's father's father, Dmitri Nikolaevich Nabokov, Minister of Justice under Alexander II and Alexander III, had had his rooms. The town house was a wedding present to Nabokov's mother, Elena Ivanovna Rukavishnikov, from her parents. The Rukavishnikovs were an extremely wealthy family (their fortune came from mines in the province of Perm on the eastern flank of the

opposite *Nevsky prospekt in the early 1900s. St Petersburg's main thoroughfare, which runs from the Admiralty to the Aleksandr Nevsky Monastery.*

below The Nabokovs' town house, 47 Bolshaya Morskaya, St Petersburg. The gateway leading to the rear courtyard and garage is immediately to the left of the entrance. Nabokov's father's study (with curtain at the window and ironwork decoration above) and Nabokov's mother's sitting room (with oriel window) were on the first floor; the children's rooms were on the second floor.

St Petersburg inner town, showing:

1 Nabokov town house, now Nabokov Museum, 47 Bolshaya Morskaya Street

2 Tenishev School, 33–5 Mokhovaya

3 Tauride Palace (Tavrichesky dvorets), seat of the State Duma from 1906 to 1917.

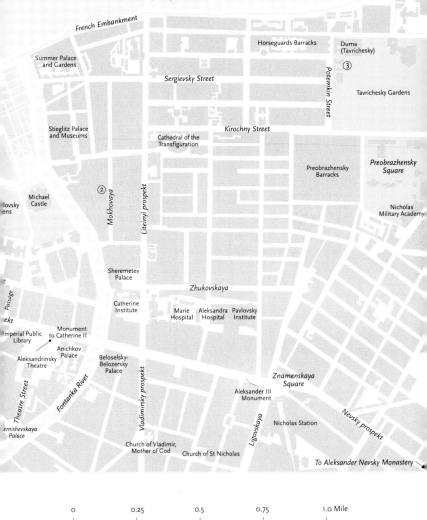

To Finland Station

Aleksandrovsky Bridge

French Embankment

Summer Palace
and Gardens

Horseguards Barracks

Duma
(Tavrichesky)
③

Sergievsky Street

Tavrichesky Gardens

Potemkin Street

Stieglitz Palace
and Museums

Kirochny Street

Cathedral of the
Transfiguration

Preobrazhensky
Barracks

Preobrazhensky
Square

Michael
Castle

②

Mokhovaya

Literinyi prospekt

Nicholas
Military Academy

Sheremetev
Palace

Zhukovskaya

Catherine
Institute

Marie
Hospital

Aleksandra
Hospital

Pavlovsky
Institute

Passage

Imperial Public
Library

Monument
to Catherine II

Anichkov
Palace

Aleksandrinsky
Theatre

Beloselsky-
Belozersky
Palace

Znamenskaya
Square

Theatre Street

Fontanka River

Vladimirsky prospekt

Aleksander III
Monument

Ligovskaya

Nevsky prospekt

ernishevskaya
Palace

Nicholas Station

Church of Vladimir,
Mother of God

Church of St Nicholas

To Aleksander Nevsky Monastery

0   0.25   0.5   0.75   1.0 Mile

above Nabokov's grandparents. **a** *Nabokov's father's father, Dmitri Nikolaevich Nabokov (1826–1904).* **b** *Nabokov's father's mother, Maria Ferdinandovna Nabokov (1842–1926), née Baroness von Korff.* **c** *Nabokov's mother's father, Ivan Vasilievich Rukavishnikov (1841–1901).* **d** *Nabokov's mother's mother, Olga Nikolaevna Rukavishnikov (1845–1901), née Kozlov.*

below *Vyra. The house owned by Nabokov's parents where Nabokov spent most of his summers as a child. View from the garden.*

After the Revolution the house served as a veterinary school in the 1920s and 1930s, and as a German staff HQ during the Second World War. It was burned down in 1944 as the Germans retreated from the area.

opposite *Nabokov's sketch-map of the three family estates of Vyra, Rozhdestveno (Nabokov preferred the older spelling 'Rozhestveno') and Batovo clustered round the Oredezh River and its tributary the Grezna.*

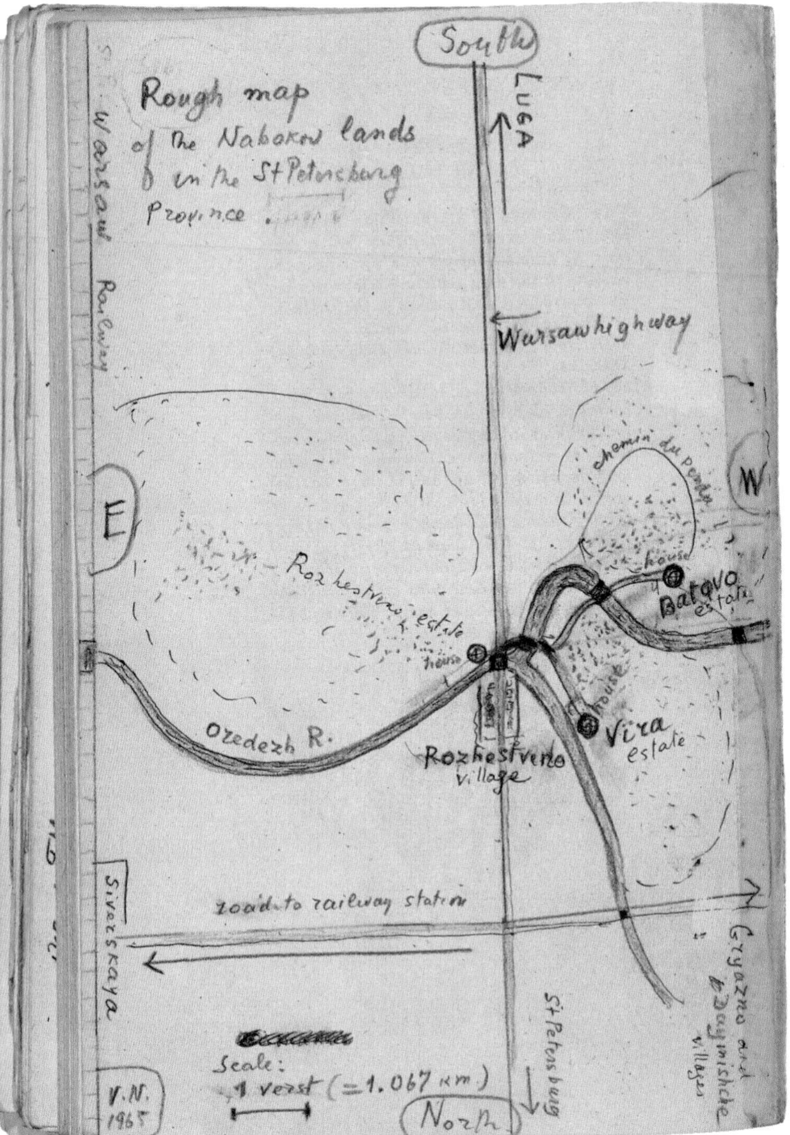

Rough map
of the Nabokov lands
in the St Petersburg
Province.

South

Luga

Warsaw Railway

Warsaw highway

chemin du Peuple

W

E

house

Batovo
estate

Rozhestveno estate

house

house

Vira
estate

Ozeredzh R.

Rozhestveno
village

road to railway station

Siverskaya

St Petersburg

Gryazno and
to Daymishche
village

Scale:
1 verst (= 1.067 km)

North

V.N.
1965

Urals), with, on the grandmother's side (the Kozlovs), a distinguished academic background. The Rukavishnikov estates outside St Petersburg at Rozhdestveno and Vyra adjoined that of Batovo, belonging to Nabokov's paternal grandmother, Maria Ferdinandovna Nabokov (née von Korff). It was here in the country that Nabokov's parents had met, and Nabokov's father had proposed to Elena Ivanovna on a bicycle ride through the Vyra estate. There were books at Vyra too where the family regularly spent the summers from May to September – books on entomology and generations of children's books in the schoolroom upstairs, old favourites like the *Arabian Nights* and Malory's legends of King Arthur and his Knights, the stirring Wild West adventures by Mayne Reid, and the exploits of the Scarlet Pimpernel, Phileas Fogg and Sherlock Holmes.

above *Rozhdestveno. This late-eighteenth-century wooden mansion and the surrounding two-thousand-acre estate belonged in Nabokov's childhood to his Uncle Vasily Rukavishnikov, who bequeathed it to him on his death in 1916.*

opposite *Nabokov's mother and father at Vyra, 1905. A rare glimpse of Vyra in wintertime, when the disturbances in the capital persuaded Nabokov's father to take his family to the country.*

Nabokov's father was especially fond of Dickens and would read aloud to his children. But Nabokov's cherished childhood memory is of the bedtime stories his mother read to him in English in the drawing room. He remembers in particular the fairy tale of a little boy who stepped out of his bed into a picture and rode his hobby-horse along a painted path in a dense European beechwood. He does not name the story, but the detail of a boy climbing out of his bed into a picture of a landscape brings to mind Hans Andersen's well-known tale of 'The Sandman'. Nabokov recalls it in association with a watercolour that hung above his bed. As he knelt and said his English prayers ('Gentle Jesus meek and mild . . .') he would imagine climbing into the picture and plunging into that enchanted forest. Less than twenty years later he was to do just that. All too soon the journey of the imagination was to become the journey of reality. Yet in focusing on this image in later life Nabokov was also tracing the pattern of a further journey – through lived experience into the enchanted world of his own art. It is a sequence that is repeated over and again. The loves and adventures and derring-do first encountered second-hand in books later become part of his own experience, and then are reworked in fiction. A paradigm of the writer's life: art to life to art.

Nabokov's thrice-told autobiography, *Speak, Memory*, is the best source for an account of his childhood, and not only for the obvious reason that for much it is the only source, and revealing in what it chooses not to write about as well as in what it does, but also because it poses the very questions that a reader of his literary biography seeks answers to: What made me what I am? And what equipped me for the life of a writer in exile?

His was not just an extremely wealthy but also an exceptionally cultivated family. Both Nabokov's parents were perfectly at ease in English and French, and both knew German. As Russians of that class and education did, they switched language codes unselfconsciously in everyday conversation. The autobiography has a nice example of this. Nabokov is eleven and beginning to ask an adolescent's awkward questions:

I soon noticed that any evocation of the feminine form would be accompanied by the puzzling discomfort already familiar to me. I asked my parents about it (they had come to Berlin to see how we were getting along) and my father ruffled the German newspaper he had just opened and replied in English (with the parody of a possible quotation – a manner of speech he often adopted in order to get going): 'That, my boy, is just another of nature's absurd combinations, like shame and blushes, or grief and red eyes.' 'Tolstoy vient de mourir,' he suddenly added, in another, stunned voice, turning to my mother.

'Da chto ti [something like 'good gracious']!' she exclaimed in distress, clasping her hands in her lap. 'Pora domoy [time to go home],' she concluded, as if Tolstoy's death had been the portent of apocalyptic disasters. (*Speak, Memory*, Chapter 10)

A succession of English and French nannies and governesses ensured that the children were fluent in English and French from early childhood, while in the summer of 1906 the services of the village schoolmaster were enlisted to ensure that Vladimir and his younger brother Sergey knew how to read and write Russian as well. Russian tutors took over later.

Language was one key that Nabokov was to pocket and use later to unlock the New World. Another, equally precious, was visual sensibility. The recognition that he thought in images and not just words was to be a source of reassurance later on when he feared he might be land-locked within the Russian language without an outlet to a reader. As a very young child it was his mother who fostered this visual sensibility by letting him play with her jewels at night, the flashing tiaras, chokers and rings, and who painted endless watercolours for him, initiating him into the mystery of how a lilac tree grew out of mixed blue and red. 'I was really born a landscape painter,' he was to tell Alfred Appel, annotator of *Lolita*, 'not a landless escape novelist as some think.' Later there were art masters who developed his sense of colour and line, including Cummings, his mother's old teacher, 'master of the sunset', and the eminent painter and graphic artist Mstislav Dobuzhinsky. Dobuzhinsky clearly exercised a lasting influence on Nabokov's artistic taste.

Throughout his life Nabokov was to retain a preference for the art of the turn of the century, especially the 'World of Art' painters, Somov, Benois and Bakst, examples of whose work he remembered hanging in the St Petersburg house and at Vyra. The location of these pictures has been uncertain for many years, but now several have resurfaced, safe and sound, in the collection of the Russian Museum, St Petersburg: among them, most importantly, the original of Bakst's pastel portrait of Nabokov's mother, two pictures of Versailles by Benois, and several sketches by Anisfeld for the ballet *Islamei*. Alas, Somov's watercolour with its rainbow, remembered by Benois and a tutor and, most touchingly, by Nabokov himself – 'young birch trees, the half of a rainbow – everything very melting and moist' (*Speak, Memory*, Chapter 11) – has not yet come to light, and though old catalogues tantalizingly list a watercolour by

Somov, '"Der alte Teich" ("The Old Pond", 1897), property of Frau Nabokoff, St Petersburg', this picture has no rainbow arching over its water. The frustrated treasure-hunter can take consolation only in the pages of Nabokov's own story 'A Visit to the Museum', where again things are not what they seem.

Dobuzhinsky also taught Nabokov to depict everyday objects from memory in the greatest possible detail: a leafless tree, a post-box, a lamppost. The training was to come in handy for the precise drawings of butterfly-wing patterns and genitalia Nabokov made later at the Harvard Museum of Comparative Zoology. And his mother reinforced the lesson of memory with love when she drew her son's attention to ephemeral moments of natural beauty on her home estate at Vyra with the words, 'Now remember.'

The lessons were not forgotten. Nabokov learned to remember and to recover the memory in his writing. Today a person returning to the Rozhdestveno district needs only a clear eye to recognize instantly from his description the leafy alleys of the old park, the

curve of the slow-moving river Oredezh, the water lilies, the bank
from which the peasant girls bathed in laughter, watched from the
other side by a dense crowd of small bright-blue male butterflies.
However, more importantly and lastingly, Nabokov also recognized,
once the pain of nostalgia was eased, that he had a developed faculty of observation and imagination with which he could do more
than recall the past; he could transform the new world around him.

Had Nabokov's parents been the kind to sit down and draw up a
programme of how to nurture and develop the creative talent in
their eldest son, they could hardly have come up with a better solution. It takes a particular understanding of a child's capacity for

wonderment for a mother to decide to cheer up her convalescent charge with a surprise parcel containing a four-foot-long display model of a Faber pencil, which he had seen hanging in a window on Nevsky prospekt. Yes, the lead went all the way through the length of the wood; the curious child later drilled a hole to check. Perhaps it was to repay her generously imaginative gesture that Nabokov devoted such attention to a pencil in his next to last novel, *Transparent Things*.

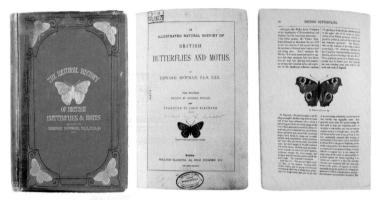

And it was Nabokov's father, busy public figure though he was, who passed on to his seven-year-old son his passion for the collection of butterflies, and the patient science of their classification. Nabokov was just nine when Vladimir Dmitrievich wrote this note to his wife (pencil on toilet paper), smuggled out from Kresty Prison where he was incarcerated for three months in 1908 for anti-government activities:

Front cover of Edward Newman's Illustrated Natural History of British Butterflies and Moths (London, 1884); title-page with Nabokov's handwritten inscription: 'coloured by Vladimir Nabokov'; and p. 60, showing a Peacock butterfly coloured by Nabokov.

Have just received your dear little letter with the butterfly from Volodya. I was very touched. Tell him that there are no butterflies here in the prison yard except rhamni *and* P. brassicae. *Have you found any* egerias?

Was Nabokov spoilt? There were five children, three boys and two girls, with just ten months separating the two eldest boys Vladimir (1899) and Sergey (1900), then Olga (1902 Old Style/1903 New Style), Elena (1906) and Kirill (1911), but while the younger four were not materially neglected it was Vladimir on whom the parents lavished most personal attention, entrusting the others more to the care of governesses and tutors. He was their favourite, and from the day that he penned his first poem his parents were among his most devoted readers. Nabokov's mother herself wrote poetry, and, while Vladimir Dmitrievich seems to have had little literary talent – he wrote a precise but plain prose – he admired it in others and encouraged it in his son.

Nabokov's parents focused on him, and he in his turn sought no other adult role models as a child. From them he derived a sure sense of self and an emotional security that stayed with him for life. And in the solipsism of youth he paid little attention to his siblings. While the age gap (three, seven and twelve years) made it understandable that he played little with his sisters and not at all with Kirill, his reluctance to make a playmate of Sergey, just ten months younger, was more marked. They had little in common as young

adimir (right) and Sergey, mmer 1906.

children: Vladimir, self-assured, boisterous, sporty, and Sergey, quieter, more dreamy, with a talent for music and a bad stutter. Nabokov was to carry the feeling of discomfort with this relationship into adult life and into his books. The unease was compounded by the discovery that Sergey was homosexual. It was the sixteen-year-old Vladimir who found a page in Sergey's diary and showed it 'in stupid wonder' to his tutor who promptly showed it to their father. Sergey's tragic death in a German concentration camp in 1945 left Nabokov no opportunity to do more than remember and regret. But that came later.

Nabokov's preferred summer playmate as a child and role model as a teenager was his cousin Yuri Rausch von Traubenberg who, sixteen months older, was ahead of him in daring, in the composition of poetry, and in girls. However, in another instance of imagination anticipating reality, their adventurous childhood games inspired by the Mayne Reid books and Fenimore Cooper turned into dress rehearsals for Yuri's own death. Yuri came from a military family – his father and grandfather before him were both generals – and he followed his father in enlisting in a cavalry regiment. He was killed in action in the early days of the Civil War in 1919.

In January 1910 Nabokov was enrolled at the Tenishev School, an egalitarian, educationally progressive establishment, with an excellent academic reputation, and some first-rate teachers. Judging by the school reports Nabokov did well, but did not over-exert himself as a pupil. He had consistently excellent reports for drawing, but made uneven progress in German and mathematics. However, the emphasis placed on sport (he played goalkeeper in the school team, which participated in a city football league) and on the natural sciences suited him, and he certainly applied himself more than Sergey who was enrolled a year later in January 1911, but who by 1915 was receiving such unsatisfactory reports that his father removed him and transferred him to his own old school, the First Gymnasium.

In later life Nabokov was to recall his school years with some warmth, and there is no evidence of his having any of the wretched experiences he gave to boys in his fiction, in *The Defense* or *Bend*

Cover of *The Headless Horseman: A Strange Tale of Texas (London, 1866) by Captain Mayne Reid (1818–83).*

Sinister. However, school was the first time where, unprotected by the home environment, he found himself exposed to the way other people thought and behaved. There were some extremely favourable comments in reports sent home to his father, as in that for the 1913/14 semester where the fourteen-year-old is described as enjoying the respect of his peers and praised not just for his footballing skills and application, but also for his 'moral decency'. However, he also came in for a good deal of ribbing from teachers and classmates, which in his autobiographical account is controlled by ironic distance, but comes across as a good deal sharper in independent records lodged in the school archive. Some frank comments by teachers kept there are revealing: 'I don't like him, he's a loner, no sense of community spirit' (woodwork); 'He is a complete mystery to me. There is style, but no substance' (political economy). These comments did not find their way into the home reports, and Nabokov may have been spared this bluntness, but he does recall being criticized for being a show-off (for peppering his Russian essays with English and French phrases), and a spoilt little rich kid (letting himself be delivered to school in a chauffeur-driven car – the choice being between the Benz or the Wolseley – rather than taking the bus or tram like other boys). In this, as in so many things, Nabokov was very much his father's son. Nabokov senior never considered his democratic political views at odds with the trappings of wealth or his aristocratic tastes. This was something picked up on by the writer Korney Chukovsky who, coming from much humbler social origins, summed up Vladimir Dmitrievich as a 'toff' ('Da, eto barin') who would arrive at the editorial offices of the liberal paper *Rech'* (*Speech*) by car, who kept a cook and had a subscription to the opera, and whose splendid suits and ties were objects of general envy and emulation. Vladimir Dmitrievich would have been amused by this last detail, to judge by a letter he wrote to his son at Cambridge in 1920 from the house of Prince Dolgorukov in Paris: 'he [Dolgorukov] categorically insists on my wearing only black ties, and made me a present of one, saying that I should give all my coloured ones away to my sons'.

In his last two years at school Nabokov was entirely taken up with the writing of poetry and an intense love affair with a girl eight months younger than he, Valentina Shulgina, whom he had met in the country when her family had rented a dacha there in the summer of 1915. He knew her as 'Liussya', but in his autobiography she appears as 'Tamara' and in his first novel as 'Mashenka', Mary. The romance continued into the winter months in Petrograd and entailed a good deal of truancy for trysts in local museums, cinemas and the nearby Tauride Palace Gardens. The following summer he had a first poem, 'Moonlight Reverie', appear in the prominent literary journal *Vestnik Evropy* (*Messenger of Europe*), and he himself published a collection of sixty-seven lyrics just a month before, in June 1916. The booklet itself was a modest enough affair, entitled simply *Stikhi* (*Poems*) and printed on ordinary paper with a cream

top *Valentina Shulgina ('Liussya')*, Nabokov's first love, 1916.
bottom *Front cover of* Stikhi *(Poems) by V. V. Nabokov, 1916.*

paper cover and minimal ornament, but there was
nothing modest about the gesture of a seventeen-
year-old schoolboy bringing out an edition of his
own work at his own expense (500 numbered
copies). It was later that same year that the young Nabokov's financial independence was more than assured when his uncle Vasily
Rukavishnikov died, bequeathing him the manor house and two-
thousand-acre estate at Rozhdestveno, and a fortune. The literary
début and the precociousness of this teenager did not go un-
noticed by his Russian literature teacher Vladimir Gippius (cousin
of Zinaida Gippius and a poet in his own right) – someone for
whom Nabokov had a great respect both as a man and a poet.
When school was back in session Gippius brought a copy of
Nabokov's volume of poems into class and deflated the preten-
sions of both the young versifier and the young lover by mercilessly
dissecting its trite and derivative clichés.

Looking back Nabokov acknowledged the justice of these criticisms with wry humour. However, there was another of Gippius's
strictures, which he never took heed of but asserted as an article of
faith, and that concerned his indifference to civic issues and refusal
to join in any of the school political debates. His response in his
final year to being asked to discuss the 1825 Decembrist uprising in
the light of the Revolutionary events of 1905 and February 1917
earned, Nabokov told his biographer Andrew Field, his teacher's
heartfelt reproach: 'You are no Tenishev boy!'

A glance at the Tenishev School magazine, *Yunaya mysl'* (*Young
Thought*), shows how just this criticism was. The seventh issue,
which appeared early in 1916, is filled with patriotic fervour and
touching idealism. Nabokov's schoolfellows press the necessity of
keeping up the war effort ('We can be defeated only by our own
faintheartedness!') and, citing Nelson, urge the setting up of a
cadet force in the school: 'Russia expects that every man will do his
duty!' Nabokov's name actually appears at the end of this issue as
one of the four editors, yet his sole identifiable contribution is a
stunningly proficient verse translation of Musset's romantic poem
'Nuit de décembre', dedicated to his girlfriend: 'for V. Sh.'.

The position Nabokov adopted then and maintained throughout his life is remarkable, given not

just the times, but his father's political prominence and record of public service. The drama which unfolded in St Petersburg in the early years of the last century was not just a backdrop to Nabokov's childhood, it was in part quite literally played out in his own home, and the young Nabokov had first-hand experience and understanding of it.

Later in emigration Nabokov was to discover that the average Westerner had a simplistic understanding of Russian history, seeing the conflict of the early years of the centrury in crude red-and-white terms, as between Bolsheviks versus diehard monarchists, and ignoring the many shades of political opinion in between, in particular the strength and influence of the liberal opposition movement in the early years of the century.

Nabokov's father, Vladimir Dmitrievich (1870–1922), trained as a lawyer like his own father, and initially opted for an academic career, but it was not long before his liberal sympathies drew him into politics. In the early years of the new century the liberal reform movement was gaining strength. In November 1904, a first national congress of *zemstvos* (elected local assemblies) convened in St Petersburg. The final session which called for a constitution, a legislative assembly and guaranteed civil rights, was held in the Nabokov town house at 47 Morskaya. It was out of these *zemstvo* groupings that the Constitutional Democratic Party (Kadets for short) was to be formed the following year.

But there were other pressures being exerted on the government, and political discontent was becoming increasingly vocal and violent. Ironically, the body that sparked off the widespread unrest of 1905 was organized by a supporter of the monarchy, the priest Father Gapon. On Sunday 9 January 1905 (Old Style) he led a huge demonstration of workers in St Petersburg. The plan was to march to the Winter Palace with a petition appealing for a living wage and for civil rights. However, the troops stationed in the streets panicked and opened fire. Well over a hundred people were killed and many more wounded. This incident, which became known as 'Bloody

Sunday', had dramatic consequences. More than anything it undermined the popularity of the Tsar, and contributed to a wave of lawlessness among the peasantry, and strikes, demonstrations and violence in the industrial cities. Workers set up trade unions for the first time, and among the professional classes and intelligentsia political parties were formed, of which the most prominent were the Kadets, who held an inaugural convention in Moscow in 1905, under the leadership of Pavel Milyukov, the eminent Moscow history professor.

Faced with a general strike Nicholas II finally conceded to the Kadets' demands for constitutional reform, and an elected parliament, the First State Duma, was formally opened on 27 April 1906 in the Tauride Palace. Liberal hopes were high, but they were to be shortlived. Nicholas had clearly no intention of surrendering autocratic power and in July summarily dissolved the Assembly. Vladimir Dmitrievich, together with other leading Kadet parliamentarians, repaired to Vyborg, Finland, and signed a manifesto protesting against the Duma's dissolution and calling on the country to resist conscription and taxes. The signatories were promptly deprived of all political rights, tried, and in 1908 served a short prison term.

The year 1906 marked the end of Vladimir Dmitrievich's parliamentary career, but he continued with his activities as journalist and criminologist up until the First World War. In 1915 he was mobilized, but after the February Revolution of 1917 he resigned his commission and re-entered politics, leading the Secretariat in the provisional government under Prince Lvov and Kerensky. The Bolshevik coup of October 1917 immediately removed the Kadets from positions of authority and put their lives at risk. In November Vladimir Dmitrievich sent his family south to the Crimea (the two eldest boys first, then his wife and younger children). He himself managed at the very end of the month to find a berth on a train leaving for Simferopol, the same day that a decree was issued ordering the arrest of all leading Kadets, 'the party of the people's enemies'.

In the Crimea he lived initially incognito. Then, after the Bolsheviks were temporarily driven back and the Germans withdrew, he was named Minister of Justice in the regional government in Simferopol. As the Bolsheviks broke through the White defences he, again in the nick of time, escaped with his family in April 1919, sailing via Constantinople to Athens, and thence to London.

opposite *The opening of the State Duma in the throne room of the Winter Palace, 27 April 1906. The occasion was the first on which representatives of all classes assembled in one hall. On the left, the appointees of the crown; on the right, the newly chosen representatives of the country – landowners, lawyers, merchants, nobles and peasants.*
right *Vladimir Dmitrievich Nabokov on his way to serve his three-month prison term in Kresty, May 1908.*

While these Revolutionary events unfolded the young Nabokov, by his own account, had little thought for anything but poetry, love and butterflies. In the Crimea from late 1917 to the spring of 1919 he led an active social life, took himself on a memorable solo butterfly expedition and made some excellent catches. He developed an interest in devising chess problems, and he also made a serious study of Andrey Bely's system of metrical scansion, which was to arm him for his dispute with Edmund Wilson in the years ahead. Yet he was certainly well informed of political developments, as independent accounts attest. A glance back to events in Petrograd in late 1916 makes this abundantly clear. Lazar Rozental, an ex-Tenishevite who was hired that winter to give extra coaching in maths, recalls that, while his young pupil was far more interested in talking about poetry than anything else, it was he who first told him in circumstantial detail about Rasputin's murder the very morning after it had happened. A brief study of the city map shows just how close this gruesome event was to the Nabokov home. The scene of the assassination, the Yusupov Palace, is just ten minutes' walk away across the Moika River. Yet the name of Rasputin figures nowhere in Nabokov's memoirs. Not for him the 'Where were you the day that Kennedy died?' approach of his younger cousin Nicholas Nabokov who in his memoir, *Bagazh: Memoirs of a Russian Cosmopolitan*, recalled as an impressionable thirteen-year-old seeing the stark headlines of the evening paper, 'RASPUTIN HAS DISAPPEARED', and then, after a wakeful night, catching a terrifying glimpse of a bulky form swathed in sheets lying on the divan in the study: Could it be . . . ?

Since early childhood Nabokov had lived with a parent in the public eye, in continual danger of losing his life and liberty. This may go some way towards explaining why at the time he might have looked upon the debates at school as all talk and mere child's-play, and why later he might have taken a certain pride in adopting his father's stiff upper lip in downplaying the drama of those years. He says nothing, for instance, of the fact that the family spent nearly two years from the autumn of 1906 in a rented house at 38 Sergievskaya Street when his mother, unnerved by the events of

The rented house at 38 Sergievskaya Street, where the Nabokov family lived from 1906 to 1908.

Bloody Sunday and the killing of children in Mariinskaya Square so near to home, had been unwilling to return to 47 Morskaya. He gives the house instead, with its 'naked old men straining to hold up a balcony' to the character of Luzhin's aunt in his novel *The Defense*.

In his fiction Nabokov takes his artistic revenge on the events that destroyed the stability of his world by employing mockery and distance. He makes his enemy seem ridiculously small by looking through the wrong end of a telescope; he destroys tyrants and assassins by laughter or by rendering them as unreal as film extras and stage actors. In his autobiography the artfulness lies in relegating politics to the wings of the action and the servants' quarters, while letting the illusory permanence of the endless cloudless

Vladimir Nabokov

summer days of a happy childhood hold centre stage – an enduring long table laid out of doors beneath the trees at Vyra for summer birthdays and namedays: 'nothing will ever change, nobody will ever die'. History is glimpsed as a series of snapshots, snatches of newsreel: brief footage of the Imperial royal family during the First World War, trains crammed with troops and, as young Vladimir and Liussya canoodle on the back row of the cinema, shabby prisoners of war with their dapper captors. Time and change are marked in the succession of servants and tutors: from his mother's nurse who was born a serf around 1830; to the radical village schoolmaster, Vasily Martynovich, who breathed Revolutionary fire and brimstone over the young Nabokov on country walks, 'speaking of humanity and freedom and the badness of warfare and the sad (but interesting, I thought) necessity of blowing up tyrants'; and finally to the

twice-treacherous Ustin, the town-house janitor, who spied for the Tsar's secret police and then in the winter of 1917–18 led the victorious Soviets to the jewels in the niche in the wall in the upstairs corner room where Nabokov was born.

In his mind's eye Nabokov sees the changes in people's attire and in the modes of transport. There is his mother in sealskin furs and muff in a horse-drawn sleigh with footman; his father mounting his high-saddled 'Dux' bicycle, which his valet would bring up to the door 'as if it were a palfrey' (early 1900s); his sisters almost falling out of the red family Opel Torpedo in their curiosity at seeing their brother emerge from the woods with Liussya (1915). There is his father again, now in trench coat and khaki cap, making a precise little cross over the faces of his sons before they board the train to the Crimea; and Nabokov himself dressed in the uniform of an officers' training school, having exchanged clothes with Yuri, in eery counterpoint to the plot of *The Headless Horseman*.

The final sight Nabokov gives of Russia is a closing-lens shot of

Opel Torpedo 1911

top, left *Model of an Opel Torpedo 1911, as owned by the Nabokov family before the Revolution.* 'And another time, as we [Nabokov and his girlfriend Valentina Shulgina] emerged onto a turn of the highway, my two little sisters in their wild curiosity almost fell out of the red family 'torpedo' swerving toward the bridge.' *(Speak, Memory, Chapter 12)*

below, left *Yuri Rausch von Traubenberg in uniform.* 'I suddenly see myself in the uniform of an officers' training school: we are strolling again villageward, in 1916, and (like Maurice Gerald and doomed Henry Pointdexter [characters from *The Headless Horseman*] have exchanged clothes – Yuri is wearing my white flannels and striped tie [. . .] And three years later [. . .] he was killed [. . .] I saw him dead in Yalta, the whole front of his skull pushed back by the impact of several bullets [. . .] in the act of recklessly attacking alone a Red machine-gun nest.' *(Speak, Memory, Chapter 10)*

Августѣйшія Дѣти ИХЪ ИМПЕРАТОРСКИХЪ ВЕЛИЧЕСТВЪ.

top The five Romanov children, c. 1910 (from left to right): Grand Duchess Tatiana, Grand Duchess Anastasia, the Tsarevich Aleksey, Grand Duchess Maria, Grand Duchess Olga.

Five children who did not survive the Revolution and who were shot, together with their parents, Nicholas and Alexandra, in Ekaterinburg, July 1918.
above The five Nabokov children in Yalta, November 1918 (from left to right): Vladimir, Kirill, Olga, Sergey, Elena (holding the dachsund, Box II).

himself and his father playing chess on the deck of the ship *Nadezhda* (*Hope*) as it steams out of Sebastopol harbour under fire from the Bolshevik guns – a last visual metaphor for quiet bravery and the triumph of hope over adversity. It is a studied yet moving ending to the account of his Russian years.

Nabokov never questioned or rebelled against his father's political beliefs. After his father's murder he donned his mantle of integrity and honour, and adhered to his liberal creed to the end of his days. Yet he never felt the need to campaign for these beliefs. It was as though his father had taken care of that side of things for him. The commitment and idealism and active involvement that jump fresh off the pages of his father's writings are not things that Nabokov ever shared in. This confident and ambitious son of a famous father from the very beginning set his course for another shore.

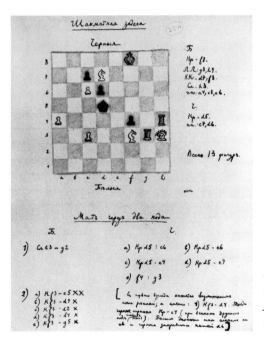

A chess problem composed by Nabokov: 'Mate in two moves', from his Crimea notebook (February–June 1919).

Europe: 1919–1940

SIRIN

> *Tossing back its thick curls' waves,*
> *Flinging back its head,*
> *Filled with joỳ, the Sirin gazes,*
> *Filled with otherworldly bliss.*
>
> > (From Aleksandr Blok, 'The Sirin and The
> > Alkonost: Birds of Joy and Sorrow', 1899)

> *In modern times* sirin *is one of the popular Russian names of*
> *the Snowy Owl, the terror of tundra rodents, and is also*
> *applied to the handsome Hawk Owl, but in old Russian*
> *mythology it is a multicolored bird, with a woman's face and*
> *bust, no doubt identical with the 'siren', a Greek deity, trans-*
> *porter of souls and teaser of sailors. In 1920, when casting*
> *about for a pseudonym and settling for that fabulous fowl, I*
> *still had not shaken off the false glamour of Byzantine imagery*
> *that attracted young Russian poets of the Blokian era.*
> > (*Strong Opinions*, Interview 1970)

In October 1919 Nabokov enrolled at Trinity College, Cambridge.
He started out studying zoology, but switched to the modern languages tripos after two terms and read for a degree in French and
Russian, like his brother Sergey who, after an unhappy first term
at Oxford, transferred to Christ's College, Cambridge.

Nabokov's father initially planned for the whole family to stay in
England and to make London the base for his resumed political
activity, together with Pavel Milyukov. He and Milyukov jointly
brought out an English-language weekly, *The New Russia*. However,
their political differences widened and Milyukov moved to make
Paris the centre of his operations, where he became editor of the

main émigré left-wing daily, *Poslednie novosti* (*Latest News*). Nabokov's father, though reluctant to leave England, which he found much more congenial (it helped that his brother Konstantin was chargé d'affaires at the London Embassy at the time), nevertheless could see that there was no political future for him in London and accepted the invitation of his old friend Iosif Hessen to join him in Berlin and become editor of the new liberal daily he was setting up, *Rul'* (*The Rudder*). So the family moved to Germany, leaving the elder boys to continue their studies at university.

above *The Sirin bird: inspiration for Nabokov's Russian literary pseudonym. From a mid-nineteenth-century* lubok, *a Russian popular print.*

opposite *Nabokov as an undergraduate at Trinity College, Cambridge, November 1919.*

Thus far, superficially at least, things had not turned out so very differently from planned. It had always been envisaged that Vladimir and Sergey would complete their studies at Oxford or Cambridge. Nabokov had not had his schooling interrupted (although admittedly he had taken his last exams a couple of months early). He had not been conscripted, nor joined the White army. Instead, in today's parlance, what had he had? – an extended gap year in the Crimea. And here he was slipping into the quaint routine of the Cambridge student: the chapel bells and bicycles, draughty wainscoted rooms, muffins toasted on a smoky open fire, the river, the meadows, the grass tennis courts, the sodden football pitches. Except that there *had* been a war, there *had* been a Revolution, Yuri was dead and so were a good many of his schoolfellows, while Liussya, Vyra and, indeed, Russia itself, were lost for ever. He felt as though a glass wall separated him from the world around him. His English surroundings seemed as artificial as the trappings of his Anglophile childhood, purchased, like the Pears Soap, the Huntley & Palmer's Biscuits, the striped jersey of a public school he never attended (he gives this unwanted jersey to his character Martin in *Glory*), from Drew's English shop on Nevsky prospekt. Reality was the Russia that he had lost, and it was this acute consciousness of being

Nabokov on a rowing boat on the Cam, 1920: 'It turned out that in Cambridge there are a whole number of the simplest things which a student traditionally must not do. It is not done, for example, to go on the river in a rowing-boat – hire a canoe or a punt instead.' *(From Nabokov's Russian essay entitled 'Kembridzh', published in* Rul´, *28 October 1921.)*

Russian that he wanted to cling on to. The part of him that wanted to write did not want it any other way.

Thus it was perfectly true, as Nabokov writes in *Speak, Memory*, that the story of his university years in England was really the story of his trying to become a Russian writer. Yet, while he did socialize with the Russian set and, predictably, his closest friends were Russians, he led in most other respects the typical life of an English undergraduate. He worked moderately hard, and he played hard – football (keeping goal for Trinity, as he had at the Tenishev), tennis, student pranks – besides enjoying an active social life outside the university through his uncle's Russian and English contacts in London. He saw a good deal of a young woman five years older than he, Eva Lubrzynska, with whom he had been romantically involved in Petrograd in 1917 and who – small world – he met by chance at a London ball and whose brother was at Peterhouse. In 1920 she was to marry a Trinity friend of his, son of the architect Edward Lutyens. He even in his first term stepped out of character and took part in a political debate at the Trinity Magpie and Stump Debating Society. He spoke against the motion 'That this House approves of the Allied Policy in Russia', using an English-language article by his father, which he had memorized for the occasion. Unsurprisingly, he dried up after eighteen minutes when he had run out of what he had learned off by heart, 'and that', he commented afterwards, 'was my first and last political speech'.

Loss was his first theme as an émigré writer, and he trained his memory and his inner eye on the recall of the irrecoverable perfect past. He dreamed of Russia constantly; he recrossed the borders over and over in his imagination, wringing every drop of poetry from it. He entitled a verse volume he began in his third term

Title-page of notebook of verse entitled 'Nostalgia: Stikhi' (April 1920–July 1921).

Nostalgia and made this the subject of his first story, 'The Wood-Sprite', where he imagines being visited in his exile by an elfin spirit from the old park at Vyra who has fled, as the trees have been chopped down, and travelled across a Russia filled with devastation and rotting corpses. He never seriously thought of returning to Russia, nor of recontacting his lost love Liussya. Instead he recovered her in his first novel, *Mashen′ka (Mary)*, where his hero lets her go for ever, while in two other stories he invoked the myth of Orpheus and Eurydice, with its stern warning: 'Don't look back.' In later life he was to overcome this nostalgia and when asked in an interview in 1969 if he ever had a longing for *one* place, for 'a scrap of Russia in return for the whole of the United States', he replied simply: 'I have no such longings.' First, though, he had to feel the acute exquisite pain.

Much of this early writing, and it was mainly poetry, was derivative and laden with sentiment, but from the start the focus of his recall was sharp. He never indulged in the recreation of an artificial kitsch 'Russia abroad', with its décor of lacquered boxes and figured porcelain of the kind he gives to Luzhin's in-laws in *The Defense*, nor looked through the rose-tinted spectacles of his French governess, Cécile Miauton. She had been extemely unhappy in Russia and yet wiped this completely from her memory once she returned to her native Switzerland, and merely replaced the picture postcard of the Château de Chillon that she had kept on her writing desk in St Petersburg with the picture of a garish troika.

Nabokov's theme was loss. His medium was memory. His instrument was the Russian language. To tune and tone this precious instrument he immersed himself in Russian literature, ancient and modern, and he disciplined himself to read ten pages a day of Vladimir Dahl's four-volume Russian dictionary, which he purchased in Cambridge market-place – at least, that was his resolve.

His diet was not exclusively Russian literature. He read a great deal of French as part of his course, and outside it he read contemporary English literature, especially the Georgian poets. Cambridge had its own ghosts and its war dead. It was in Cambridge that

The poet Rupert Brooke (1887–1915) *in Royal Navy Division Uniform,* *1914; most remembered for the lines* *from his sonnet 'The Soldier' (1914):* *If I should die, think only this of me:* *That there's some corner of a foreign field* *That is forever England.*

Nabokov came across the poetry of Rupert Brooke and blended the image of his untimely death in the First World War with the image of his cousin Yuri. He translated all or parts of twenty poems in preparing an essay he sent to his parents in September 1921. 'Rupert Bruk', appeared the following year in the first issue of the Berlin émigré miscellany *Grani* (*Borders*) – his first published piece of literary criticism. And it was also at Cambridge that he first encountered the work of James Joyce, recalling his fellow undergraduate Peter Mrosovsky bursting into his room with a copy of *Ulysses* freshly smuggled from Paris; though his real reading of Joyce, as of Proust, came only later in the 1930s.

Looking back on his Cambridge years Nabokov remembers them dominated by the morbid fear of losing the purity and flexibility of his Russian language, of having it corrupted by alien influence. However, while his reading of literature in English undoubtedly left its mark on the Russian poetry he was writing at this time, his fears of losing his

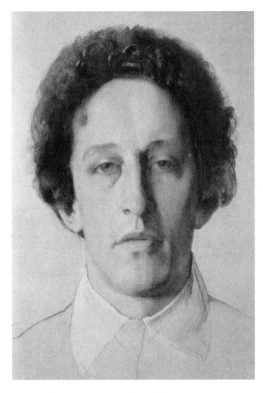

left *Aleksandr Blok (1880–1921), portrait by K. A. Somov (1907). Blok, Russia's most famous Symbolist poet, died aged just forty in Petrograd, 7 August 1921. The young Nabokov was a great admire of his verse and wrote two poems in his memory (published in* Rul´, *14 August and 20 September 1921). On 17 September, he had joined his father in paying tribute at a memorial evening organized by the Union of Russian Journalists and Writers i Berlin.*

opposite *Sketches made by Pushkin of his friend the poet Kondratii Ryleev, and of hanged men, following the execution of leaders of the Decembrist uprising in July 1826. Pushkin had been clos to several of the conspirators, and was haunted by the hangings for some years afterwards.*

Note: The 'Chemin du pendu' ir the Batovo park, where local legend had it that a pistol duel between Ryleev and Pushkin took place in 1820, is marked by Nabokov on his sketch-map of the family estates (s p. 17).

Russian heritage were unfounded. As Nina Berberova, a close contemporary and fellow writer, astutely observed, among émigré writers Nabokov was one of the lucky few who was old enough to have left Russia not empty-handed but with a solid grounding in Russian culture, and yet young enough not to be forever stuck in the rut of nostalgia, forever looking backwards with only Russia as his theme. Nabokov's faithful companion in exile, the old travelling-bag that had transported what was salvaged of his mother's jewels out of Russia, though now emptied of its tangible treasure, yet remained full of inalienable property: Blok, Bely, Mandelshtam, Pasternak; Pushkin,

Gogol, Turgenev, Tolstoy and Chekhov. Nabokov had walked the same streets of St Petersburg as Pushkin and Gogol, and trodden the same paths as the poet Ryleev, the doomed Decembrist whose family had owned Batovo in the early nineteenth century and who, so the story went, had duelled there with Pushkin. All this cultural baggage Nabokov carried with him into exile; but he did not only have the past, he also had the present, and he had a future.

He was fortunate too in not finding himself abroad alone, but together with all his immediate family, including the one surviving grandparent, Maria Nabokov, and in being able to rely on his parents' complete understanding and support. He would bombard them with poems in his letters. His mother would copy them out. His father would respond with his usual mix of banter, chess problems, understated encouragement ('Your last poems aren't bad'), gentle reminders not to neglect his studies ('no danger of mental exhaustion. Not for you at any rate – although two hours of work a day is a terrible load: . . . 7,200 seconds a day!') and fond humour (signing off a letter in May 1921 with this affectionate greeting from an expansive Slav to the land of the stuffed shirt: 'And lots of big kisses on the lips right in the middle of Cambridge').

Edition of Rul´, Thursday 30 Marc
1922, with a heavy black border, ca
rying the announcement of the tra
gic death of its editor, Vladimir
Dmitrievich Nabokov.

It was his father he had to thank, and Iosif Hessen, for his early
and easy entry into the pages of *Rul´*, which was widely respected
throughout the emigration as a leading cultural, and not just narrowly political, publication. Here he published his first poems and
prose and made his début as 'Vladimir Sirin'. It was a pseudonym
chosen not with the intention of concealing his identity, but merely
to distinguish himself from his father – *sirin* being a fabulous bird
of paradise of Russian folklore, and the colourful emblem of a
Symbolist publishing house in turn-of-the-century St Petersburg.

And then his father was dead. On 28 March 1922 Vladimir

Dmitrievich Nabokov was assassinated at a public meeting in Berlin. He had invited Milyukov over from Paris to speak. The bullets fired by the two Russian monarchist extremists were intended for Milyukov. Yet it was Vladimir Dmitrievich who was fatally wounded as he went to his friend's defence. Young Vladimir was home for the Easter vacation before the Cambridge final examinations. His mother was laying out cards for patience and he was reading aloud a poem of Blok's. The phone rang and Nabokov answered it. It was Hessen. The tragedy shook the entire émigré community. Political differences were forgotten in the remembrance of a man of absolute integrity. As Chukovsky put it in that rather Russian way: 'He was the purest of men.'

For the Nabokovs it meant quite simply the break-up of the family unit. Elena Ivanovna, Nabokov's mother, now left without financial support, accepted the offer of a small pension from the Czech government and moved to Prague in October 1923. Her daughters and Kirill joined her there, while Sergey made his base in Paris. Nabokov meanwhile, after the funeral on 1 April, went back to Cambridge to sit his exams and get his degree, then left England for good and returned to Germany. He could afford to visit his mother only rarely in the 1920s and 1930s, and was never able to support her as he would have liked. She never returned to Berlin, and died in Prague in May 1939. He was unable to go to her funeral.

Nabokov was devastated by the death of his father, and was to return to it again and again in his writing. But his life moved on. In the space of just over a year he was engaged to be married (June 1922 to Svetlana Siewert, the seventeen-year-old daughter of a wealthy mining engineer whom he had met the previous summer), had the engagement broken off by his fiancée (January 1923, her parents having made it clear that a young man without a steady job, a mere scribbler, was not a suitable match for their daughter), went through acute pains of rejection, wrote streams of poems, met (May 1923) and fell in love with the woman who was to become his wife (Véra Evseevna Slonim), and had his first four

opposite *Nabokov with his fiancée,*
Svetlana Siewert, Berlin 1922.
above *Elena Ivanova Nabokov.*
Nabokov's own inscription to this
photograph reads: 'Mother in her
twelfth year of exile, Prague 1931.'

books published: two books of verse and two of translation, one of them of Lewis Carroll's *Alice in Wonderland*. In Iosif Hessen (1865–1943), the publisher who saw these books into print, and the eminent critic Yuly Aikhenvald (1872–1928) who gave him his first favourable review, Nabokov found good geniuses, supportive father figures who, together with the poet Khodasevich (1886–1939) whom he met later in Paris, were to combine to form the composite character of the writer Koncheev in *The Gift*. In Véra he was to find a lover, a loyal wife and good mother to his son, a lifetime companion and his best reader. He was never to be alone again.

Véra Slonim was two years younger than he, also from St Petersburg, also from an educated cultured background, but not nearly as privileged or wealthy as Nabokov's, and Jewish. She too felt unsettled and alone in Berlin. Her father and mother split up

some time in 1924, her father moved in with a considerably younger relative of his wife, Anna Feigin, and for a time divided loyalties drove wedges between Véra and her two sisters. Both parents died soon after in 1928. Véra was a very attractive young woman, and Nabokov too was very good-looking in his twenties and thirties. They made, as they say, a lovely couple. But from the outset it was not just the man, but the poet in the man that attracted Véra. She had already admired him from his public readings given in 1921–2, and kept cuttings of his poems, and for Nabokov it was the stuff of story-book romance for him to meet his wife-to-be at a ball, for her to be wearing a mask, and for her to recite his verse to him. Nabokov may well have artistically reworked this memory; it may not have been at a ball, nor on 8 May, the day that entered family lore, yet there certainly was a meeting on a bridge where Véra wore a black satin wolf mask. Already at the end of that month, when he is still writing soulful letters to his ex-fiancée, Svetlana, he writes to Véra: 'you are the one person I can talk to – about the line of a cloud, about the singing of a thought', and when he is in Prague visiting his mother early in 1924 he writes to Véra that she 'is among the three people who understand my every comma, and one of those [my father] is now dead'. They were married the following year on 15 April 1925.

With all her intelligence, strong-mindedness and independence, Véra never was ambitious for herself or wanted to be anything in her own right, anything other than his wife, Sirin's wife. From the very start of their life together in Berlin she did everything she could to allow him to concentrate on his writing, taking care of the everyday practical things, doing his typing and acting as his first reader. These were indigent years, lived in a succession of rented rooms, and both of them had to turn their hand to what they could to make ends meet. Véra used her knowledge of French and German to work as a translator, tourist guide and interpreter, and acquired the secretarial skills to take on a series of clerical jobs for commercial and legal firms (this provided good copy for Zina's job in *The Gift*). Nabokov never earned enough in Europe by his writing alone for them to live on. A good part of his day in the late 1920s and early

above Nabokov advertising his services as private tutor in Rul´, 2 February 1927: 'V. V. Nabokov-Sirin offers English and French language lessons.' Steinplatz 132–66 is a telephone number where he could be contacted from 2 to 3 p.m.

below Mashen´ka (Mary) by Vladimir Sirin. Front cover of Nabokov's first novel (Berlin: Slovo, 1926).

1930s was taken up with private tutoring – mostly English- and French-language lessons, but also coaching in tennis and boxing, translating, reviewing, working as a film extra, devising chess problems and the first Russian crossword puzzles, with his own writing done mainly in the evening and at night. Yet the ambition and drive were all there, as well as the application (his hard-working father need have had no fears that his son turn out a dilettante), and between the mid-1920s, when he turned his main attention from poetry to prose, to 1940, when he left Europe, he published two plays, over fifty short stories and nine novels.

What also impresses about the years just before and after his marriage is the diversity of Nabokov's interests. In the early years of the Weimar Republic, 1919–23, Berlin was the largest centre of the Russian emigration, and it remained a lively cultural and publishing centre for the Russian community even after 1923 when spiralling inflation led to the collapse of many business ventures and a mass exodus of Russians from Germany, largely to Paris, which became the capital of the diaspora. Letters to his mother in 1926 recount chess matches (including one with Alékhine, the future world champion), trips to the theatre, to Dobuzhinsky's art exhibition (he too emigrated, first to Lithuania and Western Europe, and later to the United States), and a visit to the entomology collection at Dahlem. The man who would say later in 1969 that he had 'never belonged to any literary, political or social coterie', did just that: he actively participated in several Russian literary groups and clubs. In 1923 he was a member of the Writers' Club, where – reflecting the temporary blurring of borders between Soviet and émigré Russia – Bely, Pasternak and Erenburg, Khodasevich and Victor Shklovsky all spoke and read their work. In 1926 he was even a member of an anti-Bolshevist secret society, in these cloak-and-dagger days of defections and border-crossings, espionage and counter-espionage – the world that found its way into *The Eye* and *Glory*. And he was always on the lookout for more lucrative openings for his writing talent. This was the Berlin of Kurt Weill and Bertolt Brecht, and the émigré community had a lively café and cabaret life of its own. Nabokov collaborated with a friend Ivan Lukash in 1923–4 in writing comic skits and sketches for the Russian Bluebird Café. And as the silent cinema made way for the talkies at the end of the decade he entertained ambitions of turning his works into film. Like his character Margot in *Laughter in the Dark* and like the young Lolita he was always 'mad on the movies'. Berlin in the 1920s and early 1930s was a film-maker's mecca and a film-goer's paradise. From the gothic horror of *The Cabinet of Dr Caligari* with the sinister Conrad Veidt, to the stark expressionism of Fritz Lang's *Metropolis* and Josef von Sternberg's *Blue Angel*, Nabokov saw it all, but the kind of picture he remembered liking best from these days was the

opposite *Vladimir Nabokov (seated at the front, second from left sporting the pipe) with the cast of his play* The Man from the USSR, *first performed 1 April 1927 at the newly opened émigré Group Theatre, Berlin.*

right, top *Marlene Dietrich in Josef von Sternberg's* Blue Angel *(1930).*

right, below *Harold Lloyd in* Safety Last *(1923). Nabokov introduced this shot into his novel* The Defense *(Chapter 14): Luzhin is looking at photographs in the office of Valentinov's film studio: 'And on one there was a white-faced man with lifeless features and big American glasses, hanging by his hands from the ledge of a sky-scraper – just about to fall off into the abyss.'*

American knock-about comedy of Laurel and Hardy, Buster Keaton, Harold Lloyd, the Marx Brothers and Charlie Chaplin. Many Russians found their way into films in one way or another and Nabokov did see the chance of a future in Hollywood in the early 1930s. But his contacts came to nothing and he was to wait forty years before he finally made it to California to write the filmscript for *Lolita*. Instead he fed his cinematic vision – the mime, the music-hall gags, the slapstick – into the black comedy of a work like *Invitation to a Beheading*.

While artists, writers and intellectuals were being expelled from Soviet Russia, there was also pressure put upon émigrés to return and lend prestige to the young Soviet state. And many writers did –

out of homesickness, out of patriotism. Nabokov was also approached in late 1931 through Alexander Tarasov-Rodionov, the then celebrated author of that good Communist novel *Chocolate*. He was not tempted, and it is surely no coincidence that in 1934 he made the duplicitous mad Hermann Karlovich of his novel *Despair* an agent for a chocolate-manufacturing firm.

But if the young Sirin was no recluse, his anti-herd mentality and aversion to ideology were displayed with all the forthrightness of his later years. At Aikhenvald's literary circle he did more than read from his stories and novels, he gave talks in which he inveighed against 'Generalities', against historical determinism, against the systematized psychology of Freud, against any political, social or moral concerns that distracted writers or their readers from what he judged to be the only proper business of art, which was to convey a unique way of seeing the world. Pushkin in his view was not to be totemized as a champion of freedom, nor *Eugene Onegin* to be read as an encyclopaedia of Russian social life. Gogol was not the champion of the underdog, nor was *Dead Souls* an abolitionist tract. In his own novel *The Gift* he made a devastating, and devastatingly funny, attack on the nineteenth-century socialist thinker Chernyshevsky who had done more than anyone to politicize the reading of literature. This earned him enemies among the politically conscious left for whom Chernyshevsky had quasi iconic status, and the editors of the main French émigré journal *Sovremennye zapiski* (*Contemporary Annals*) banned the chapter containing Chernyshevsky's fictionalized biography.

It was not just his irreverent attitude towards the heroes of Russia's past that made him enemies in literary circles, but also his intolerance of mediocrity in the writing of his contemporaries. He could be bitingly savage in his reviews. He could hardly expect to be forgiven for the farcical fun he made of the young novelist Yanovsky's clumsy attempt to describe a football match, nor was he. Nor did Georgy Ivanov (a talented poet) forgive Nabokov for the sarcasm with which he dismissed a novel by his wife, Irina Odoevtseva. In 1930 Ivanov reviewed all that Sirin had written over the last four years for the opening number of a new Paris journal,

Chisla (*Numbers*), and delivered the judgement that Sirin was like a smooth elegantly dressed character out of the movies, who makes out he is a count but is in reality a base-born impostor. Ivanov's review caused quite a buzz in émigré literary circles. Its lasting significance, however, lies not in its offensiveness, but in the clear indication it gave that by 1930 Sirin had arrived.

Here was not just an interesting young hopeful, but a force to be reckoned with. While Ivanov was doing his best to bury Nabokov, another contemporary, Nina Berberova, was registering, with the publication of *The Defense* in *Sovremennye zapiski*, that 'a great Russian writer, like a phoenix, was born from the fire and ashes of revolution and exile'. Friend or foe, devotee or detractor, what no one could deny was Nabokov's extraordinary talent. Soon his reputation began to outshine not only those of his contemporaries but also of writers of the older generation. Ivan Bunin was, when

The Russian writer Ivan Alekseevich Bunin (1870–1953), awarded the Nobel Prize for Literature, 1933.

Nabokov started out, the undisputed leading writer of the emigration. In 1926, before they were personally acquainted, Nabokov had sent him a copy of his first novel *Mary* with the inscription: 'I am both happy and terrified at sending you my first book. Please do not judge me too harshly.' Yet in 1933 when Bunin was awarded the Nobel Prize for Literature (he was the first Russian to receive the award, and all the Russian emigration was honoured through him), it was Nabokov's star that was in the ascendant, and by the end of the decade his success had made the ageing writer so resentful that he bridled at the very mention of the name Sirin.

Sirin's name was everywhere in the émigré literary papers and journals, while 'Nabokoff-Sirin' was also beginning to become known outside Russian circles. German translations of his first two novels had come out in 1928 and 1930 within two years of their publication, and in the 1930s novels appeared in English and in French translation. Jean-Paul Sartre memorably – at least Nabokov never forgot – reviewed the French translation of *Despair* (*La Méprise*), calling it a 'strange miscarriage of a novel' and its author 'M. Nabokoff' completely cut off from his literary roots. A judgement lightly made, maybe, yet, in the context of Nabokov's later development, it stands out, alongside the recurrent comment in Russian émigré reviews – this while he was still writing exclusively in Russian – that his work was in some respects 'foreign', 'un-Russian'. By some he was criticized for choosing non-Russian settings and characters. Others complained that his formal and compositional brilliance was foreign to the Russian literary tradition. Still others regretted that he lacked the 'love of humanity' that had been the moving force of most great Russian writing.

Underlying these criticisms was a good measure of conservatism, a modicum of sentimentality and more than a touch of envy. And Nabokov answered them all in *The Gift*, but he did so in his own way. He made Russian literature its main subject. As he wrote in his foreword to the English translation, its true heroine is Russian literature. Every chapter is saturated with Russian literary reference. Yet a reader can easily see that Western European literature is there too: Proust and Joyce. For Nabokov never conceived of the Russian literary tradition as something narrowly nationalistic, cut off from Western Europe influences. In this his model was always Pushkin, that most European, most eclectic, yet most Russian of writers. He remained absolutely consistent over this in both his Russian and American incarnations. In his Russian novel *King, Queen, Knave*, a novel about adultery, he makes conscious play of 'amiable little imitations' of Flaubert's *Madame Bovary*. Later in his English autobiography he alludes, this time perhaps unconsciously, to the same source when he describes the departure from Russia and envisages his forsaken Liussya's letters fluttering like bewildered butterflies as they fail to reach their addressee. The

A Camberwell Beauty, the butterfly Nabokov associated with his first love, Valentina Shulgina: 'That spring of 1916 is the one I see as the very type of a St Petersburg spring, when I recall such specific images as [. . .] a Camberwell Beauty, exactly as old as our romance, sunning its bruised black wings [. . .] on the back of a bench in Alexandrovski Garden . . .' (Speak, Memory, Chapter 12)

butterflies recall his own captures, as well as the two summers of their young love, but they also bring to mind the black butterflies of Emma Bovary's burned wedding bouquet, and the white butterflies of the torn assignation note, which flutter from the window of the carriage that, with its blinds drawn, carries Emma and her lover round the streets of Rouen.

Nabokov was a cultural eclectic in most respects, but for him language was another matter entirely. Throughout his European exile, he remained filled, as when he first found himself in England, with a 'panicky fear' of flawing his Russian by contact with the alien language of his new environment. Herein lies, perhaps, an answer to the question that is often asked of his Berlin years: Why did he stay on so long in Germany? Why did he stay after 1923 when so many fellow Russians left for other émigré centres? Why did he continue to stay in the 1930s when first the economic depression and then the rise of Hitler caused many publishing houses to close down (*Rul'*, Nabokov's mainstay, folded in 1931) and created a further mass exodus of Russians, especially Russian Jews? Between 1919 and 1923 there had been half a million Russians resident in Berlin; by 1929 there were 75,000; by 1933

there were only about 10,000 left. Nabokov and Véra did think seriously of moving to Paris in the early 1930s, yet they stayed put in
Nazi Germany. Nabokov was bilingual in French and felt a real
affinity for French culture. He knew German too, and he was being
misleading when he made out otherwise later. He had had six and a
half years of German at school, as well as spending three months
in Berlin as an eleven-year-old. And he had a German grandmother
and a German ancestry, which he could trace back to the sixteenth
century. However, and this is perhaps the answer, he had no liking
for the German language, nor any affinity with the culture, and he
loathed the politics. While he might have felt at risk of losing the
purity of his Russian in a French environment, he felt at no such
risk in Germany. Obviously, there were other considerations affect-
ing the Nabokovs' decision to stay on. After 1932 they at last had a
congenial place to live, with Véra's cousin Anna Feigin at 22
Nestorstrasse, someone on hand to help with the care of their son,
Dmitri, when he was born two years later in 1934. And Véra, with
her fluent German, was able to carry on working in the 1930s after
Nabokov's other extra sources of income dried up. Added to this
there was always the pull of inertia. However, his sense of linguistic
insulation from his German surroundings could have been the key.
In Berlin he found he could work quite happily within the goldfish
bowl of the Russian-speaking community, and, like the émigré
widow of one of his stories without her hearing-aid, enjoy an 'ideal
deafness' to the world around him while walking the streets sharp-
eyed, thinking his own thoughts.

Berlin remained Nabokov's writing base for most of the 1920s
and 1930s, but there were occasional sorties outside Germany to
visit his mother in Prague, and three reading tours to Belgium and
France in 1932, 1936 and 1937, with the conquest of Paris, now the
capital of the Russian literary world, their chief object. And he con-
quered. Each visit was more successful than the last, and the 1937
readings were a sell-out, with rave reviews in the émigré press. If he
did not endear himself to all his public with his aristocratic St
Petersburg drawl and 'English' arrogance, everyone was agreed that
he dazzled, he shone. Even the ever critical Georgy Adamovich con-

ceded the brilliance and the polish of the delivery, while the kindly older writer Aldanov judged that if only his works could be adequately translated Sirin would take his deserved place as a world-ranking writer. Prophetic words, written just months before Nabokov's own English version of *Despair* came out in London.

On the second trip in early 1936 he gave readings to French-speaking audiences as well as Russian. In readiness for this he wrote a story in French about his governess, 'Mademoiselle O'. Already he was recognizing the need to find a wider audience, but when he left Berlin in January 1937 it was with a more specific aim than just to boost his sales and reputation. He left seeking a way out of Germany for himself and his wife and young son. The event that jolted intention into action was the news in May 1936 that the extreme right-wing monarchist Vasily Biskupsky, one of the most distrusted figures in the emigration, had been named head of Hitler's Department of Emigré Affairs. Part of Biskupsky's brief was to register Russians resident in Berlin as possible translators for use during the planned attack on Russia and to identify Jews in the Russian community, and he appointed as his under-secretary Sergey Taboritsky, one of the two men convicted of the murder of Nabokov's father. That same month Véra was dismissed from her secretarial job for being Jewish.

Now at last Nabokov delayed no longer. From May 1936 he began writing letters to friends and contacts abroad – many of them Kadets or liberal sympathizers who had known or known of his father (Bernard Pares, Sergey Konovalov, Eugene Vinaver in England; Michael Karpovich at Harvard, George Vernadsky at Yale) – looking for a teaching job in a British or American university. These letters make painful reading, as Nabokov swallows his pride and admits to being unable to support his wife, aged mother and young son, then sets out his qualifications as a teacher of English and French literature, and declares his readiness to work even in 'the most provincial' American university: 'I am not afraid of living in the American backwoods.' He was to keep trying to secure a post for the next three years, with his letters registering increasing desperation. At the same time he began trying his hand at writing in

English, writing first drafts of his autobiography, and making translations of *Despair* and *Laughter in the Dark*, while, with his characteristic ability to keep several balls in the air at once, cultivating connections in the French literary world. He secured publication for his French story 'Mademoiselle O' in Jean Paulhan's *Mesures* and a commission for a centennial essay on Pushkin in French for *La Nouvelle revue française*.

PALAIS DES BEAUX-ARTS -:- BRUXELLES

JEUDI 21 JANVIER 1937, à 20,45 h^{res}

CONFÉRENCE

DONNÉE PAR

Wladimir NABOKOFF-SIRINE

Sujet : " Le Vrai et le Vraisemblable „

à l'occasion du Centenaire de la mort de Pouchkine.

Prix : 10 fr.   Salle de Conférences.

Les cartes peuvent être numérotées au Palais des Beaux-Arts, 23, rue Ravenstein, tous les jours, de 11 à 17 heures, (taxe de location : 1 franc).

«Правда и Правдоподобие» Пушкинский доклад В. Набокова, Брюссель 1937 г.
Архив З. Ш.

This essay, 'Pouchkine ou le vrai et le vraisemblable', which he also gave as a lecture in Brussels and Paris, was about the translatability of Pushkin and included sample French translations of some of the famous lyrics. However, it was more than a French-language training exercise and an act of homage to Russia's greatest poet. In it Nabokov delivered his *profession de foi*, declaring that the artist's duty, no matter how great the temptation to speak out, is to remain aloof from tragic events of his time, 'even if the clamour of the times, the cries of the murdered victims and the growling of the brute tyrant reach his ears'. In his flat on Nestorstrasse Nabokov had heard Hitler's voice from the rooftop loudspeakers;

Véra had witnessed the first nocturnal bookburnings in Opernplatz. Now, in 1937, when his father's murderer had been put in charge of his fate, the enemy was at the gates, and he clearly felt he had the moral right to adopt that position of silent defiance. He conscientiously objected to overt engagement in political polemic. Instead he used art. In 1934 he had already responded with the novel *Invitation to a Beheading*, and in 1937 and 1938 he published two more Russian stories with a totalitarian theme, 'Cloud, Castle, Lake' and 'Tyrants Destroyed', characteristically splicing pathos with comedy and cruelty with slapstick. In the way that so often Nabokov's life imitated his art, his Paris performance of the

Pushkin lecture was not without its comic incongruity. He gave it as a last-minute stand-in for a Hungarian woman writer who had had to cancel. His émigré friends hastily gathered together something of an audience – which happened to include James Joyce. Yet some stray Hungarian sheep remained among the goats. 'A source of unforgettable consolation,' Nabokov remembered afterwards, 'was the sight of Joyce sitting, arms folded and glasses glinting, in the midst of the Hungarian football team.'

His conquest of Paris was, however, not just literary. On the 1936 visit he had been introduced to Irina Guadanini, an attractive, vivacious divorcée, three years younger than Véra, also with a fine memory for verse. She worked at the time – one of those details that are so unimportant, yet which stick in the mind – as a poodle-trimmer. In February 1937, when they met again, they embarked on a passionate affair. Hints of his roving eye occur in his letters of the 1930s to Gleb Struve and Khodasevich and it was not the first time

left *Irina Guadanini photographed in the late 1930s.*

opposite *Dmitri, aged two, Berlin 1936*: '. . . for his second birthday, he received a four-foot-long, silver-painted Mercedes racing car operated by inside pedals, like an organ, and in this he used to drive with a pumping, clanking noise up and down the sidewalk of the Kurfürstendamm while from open windows came the multiplied roar of a dictator still pounding his chest in the Neander valley we had left far behind.' (Speak, Memory, Chapter 15)

he had been unfaithful, he told Irina, yet these had been fleeting affairs and meaningless encounters. This was clearly a different situation. The involvement came at a time when Nabokov felt acutely insecure – as he had never felt before and never was to again. He had to do more than find a new base outside Germany, he had to face the fact that he had no future as a writer of Russian. For a few months he appears to have lost the plot. There does not seem to have ever been any question of his stopping loving Véra; he wrote her a letter every day, sometimes more, urging her to join him in France; he adored his young son. He was tormented by guilt. He developed severe psoriasis in February, which brought him near to suicide. In April a solicitous ill-wisher wrote Véra an anonymous letter naming Irina. Nabokov denied everything. After a good deal of indecision and prevarication they agreed to meet in Prague in May at his mother's, Véra travelling there with Dmitri, Nabokov making his way via Switzerland and Austria to avoid

setting foot in Germany. From there in July they travelled to the South of France where he at last told Véra the truth, and that the affair was not over, that he was still writing to Irina. Nabokov's letters to Irina that August told of tempestuous scenes. In September Irina visited Nabokov in Cannes and Nabokov told her it was finished. He never saw her again. Then – from both Nabokov and Véra – silence. Nabokov would not have wished Andrew Field to hear of it (but he did from another source); Véra would have denied it to his second biographer, Brian Boyd, had not the letters Nabokov wrote to Irina in 1937 survived. The photograph Nabokov chose to include in *Speak, Memory* is revealing in its reticence: a close family unit – Véra behind the camera, Nabokov and his young son in front. It is December 1937 outside their boarding-house at Menton in the South of France, and the memory it prompts is of the torment caused by the nightly visitation of mosquitoes.

This whole episode was a delicate balancing act in which the private drama was played out in counterpoint to his writing. All these

opposite *Nabokov's caption to this photograph in* Speak, Memory *(Chapter 13) reads:* 'A snapshot taken by my wife of our three-year-old son Dmitri standing with me in front of our boardinghouse, Les Hesperides, in Mentone, at the beginning of December 1937 [. . .] The winter mosquitoes, I remember, were terrible [. . .]'

right *A fantastical butterfly,* Verochka verochka, *drawn by Nabokov for Véra for Christmas 1975, and inscribed with a tender pun in a copy of the second Russian-language edition of* Dar *(The Gift) (Ann Arbor, MI: Ardis, 1975).*

Verochka verochka

for you my DAR, my darling

from V.

Montreux
Xmas
1975

months Nabokov was working on the final drafts of *The Gift*, which he finished in Menton in January 1938. This is his most autobiographical and most joyous of novels – a novel with a fairy-tale happy ending in which the hero meets his long-lost father in a dream, discovers his true path as a writer and is joined with his true love. It took tremendous creative courage on Nabokov's part to write his faith in his marriage and his future into his fiction, with Véra everywhere present and Irina nowhere – unless it is on the very last page with the lindens, and the shadow on the wall, and a poodle's unclipped claws tap-tapping over the flagstones of the night. Or else in the darkness of an unpublished sequel to the novel that he drafted a year later, which plays out the themes of betrayal and retribution and in which the hero, Fyodor, reaches the

A Nansen passport picture taken in Paris in April 1940 of Véra and five-year-old Dmitri just a month before the departure for America. The stuffed rabbit (just visible in the photograph), is, Dmitri recalls, still somewhere among his things.

cul-de-sac of his literary ambitions: 'War. An end to everything. "Tragedy of a Russian writer". And yet . . .' Here the fragment breaks off.

Nabokov wrote these grim lines in Paris in September 1939, just after war had been declared. 'And yet . . .' And yet, that same autumn came the breakthrough that he had been waiting for: a chance of a university-teaching appointment in the States. In May 1940, just weeks before the Germans entered Paris, he sailed with Véra and Dmitri for America. It was a much smaller family unit than that which had sailed from Russia twenty years earlier. His parents were dead; his sisters and brothers were dispersed in Prague, Belgium and France. But his immediate family was intact, and although he had no firm offer of a job to go to, in his travelling-bag he had ready 2,000 pages of lecture notes in English, one novel in English, *The Real Life of Sebastian Knight*, ready to be published, and some unfinished Russian business: a chapter of a novel about a palace revolution in a faraway kingdom, and a novella about the seducer of a pre-pubescent girl. *Bend Sinister*, *Lolita* and *Pale Fire* awaited the language that would bring them to life.

America: 1940–1959

I am as American as April in Arizona.
(*Strong Opinions*, Interview 1966)

In 1939, financially desperate without a work permit in France, Nabokov had pinned his hopes on finding a teaching job in an English university. 'I can't tell you how vital it is for me to find a job in England,' he had written in March 1939 to his friend Gleb Struve at the School of Slavonic and East European Studies, University of London. In all, Nabokov made three trips to England in 1937 and 1939, but nothing came of his efforts. He took his chances with America, and with his ever resilient nature he made the best of things. In May 1941 he was offered a temporary post in comparative literature at Wellesley, a private women's college in Massachusetts. Two years on he was re-hired by Wellesley to teach Russian-language courses and in 1944 appointed to a lectureship. In 1948 he took up an appointment as Professor of Russian Literature at Cornell, where he remained until the beginning of 1959. In a life that had its share of lucky breaks this needs must move to America must count as the luckiest break of all. America allowed him the existential and cultural freedom to assume a completely new identity while remaining completely himself. The Russian writer 'Sirin' was dead; the Anglo-American writer 'Vladimir Nabokov' was born.

Nabokov at Wellesley College, February 1942. The photograph prodes an apt illustration of Nabokov's itial sense of not-at-homeness on e American campus. It also gives a st image of Nabokov the lean moker. He was to give up cigarettes ree years later on his doctor's dvice after suffering heart palpita ns, and rapidly put on weight.

Yet this was not something he appreciated at the time. His initial response to his change of circumstances was to register deprivation and loss. A reader will look in vain for any sense of exhilaration at embarking on a voyage of discovery to a land of glorious new opportunity, or at embracing the challenge of a new language. He felt acutely the loss of his native language, of his reputation as a Russian writer, and of his cultural identity.

He writes poignantly of the sense of impoverishment at abandoning Russian and turning to English. It mattered not that he had known English since he was a child. Russian was not just his mother tongue, he had honed it as a creative instrument. This he saw as the essential difference between himself and another bilingual writer, Conrad, with whom he was often compared, who never wrote creatively in his native Polish before embarking on a career as a writer of English. Nabokov expresses his pain over and over in his private correspondence, and in print. His first English poem, 'Softest of Tongues', has the lines: 'And I am left to grope for heart and art/ And start anew with clumsy tools of stone'; and in his Afterword to *Lolita* he describes as his private tragedy that 'I had to abandon my natural idiom, my untrammelled, rich, and infinitely docile Russian tongue for a second-rate brand of English.'

Nabokov made his move to the United States when he had just turned forty. He was an established Russian writer with a substantial body of published work and a glittering reputation. His Russian-reading public was not large, but it was very well read, highly discriminating and passionately devoted to literature. Now he found himself a complete unknown on an American university campus, lecturing on the masterpieces of literature to the accompaniment of the clickety-click of knitting-needles from rows of female students; and dependent on the favour and patronage of well-meaning intellectuals and academics who had the most simplistic understanding of Russian politics and superficial knowledge of Russian culture. It was an enormous culture shock, a greater wrench even than he had felt when he had left Russia for Europe. In England and Germany he had thought of himself as Russian. Here in America he was made conscious of his European roots, and of the severance not just from a Russian past, but from a broader European cultural heritage. His poem 'Exile' written in 1942 is, significantly, a whimsical evocation of the out-of-placeness not of a Russian, but of a French poet on an American university campus:

He happens to be a French poet, that thin
book-carrying man with a bristly gray chin;
you meet him whenever you go
across the bright campus, past ivy-clad walls . . .

Variants of this lonely exile from Europe people Nabokov's American-based fiction: proud pedantic Pnin, mad Kinbote, Humbert Humbert, born of an English mother and a father whom he describes as a 'salad of racial genes'. These are tortured characters, trapped in an alien environment. And yet . . . how often does this phrase recur in the story of a life that has such an admirable capacity to turn losses into gains and negatives into positives? And yet . . . the works in which they appear show us not a tortured, trapped Nabokov, but an author liberating himself from linguistic and cultural taboos, and freely crossing geographical and linguistic boundaries.

Nabokov's Russian writing had a broad European cultural base; he wrote within the Westerner rather than the Slavophile Russian literary tradition; he was none the less consciously writing within a *Russian* tradition and always strenuously resisted any contamination of the purity of his Russian language. In America as a writer of English he cast aside any such inhibitions. He came to recognize linguistic and cultural interference as something beneficial and positive. His English novels are all mines, positive minefields of cross-cultural subtexts and multilingual allusions. Take *Pale Fire*, which has the poem of an American Professor of English Literature glossed by an exile from the Old-World land of Zembla; or *Ada*, with its two imaginary lands of Terra and Antiterra, and its geographical and historical blend of Old and New Worlds. He had enormous fun exploiting the richness and flexibility of the English language, as well as bending it slightly to a foreigner's ear. The brilliance of his style owes not a little to this outsider's viewpoint and while he did work at improving his facility and ironing out faults, his aim was still never to adopt a standard contemporary Anglo-American literary idiom, but always

overleaf *Nabokov with some of his Russian-language class at Wellesley College, 1944.*

to make the language his own and 'make it strange'. He hears patterns of sound and sees potential meanings that the native speaker, his perception dulled through familiarity, would simply pass over; and it is easy to spot the deliberate exploitation of Russian word-formation in his inventive use of prefixes and suffixes: 'foredream', 'forefeel', 'foreread', for example; or 'flowerlet', 'flowlet', 'beardlet', 'paper baglet', 'wartlet', 'nipplet', even 'whorelet'. He simply loved puns, much to the irritation of his self-appointed mentor, Edmund Wilson, who advised him early on: 'do please refrain from puns'. He paid him no heed and persisted in referring to *Eugene Onegin* as 'You-gin One-gin' and dubbing the hero of *Crime and Punishment* 'Rascalnikov'. And his successor at Cornell recalled him saying that the only sound he heard when he was giving his exams was the sound of underarm deodorant breaking down: 'It should be called,' he suggested, '"Speak, Mummery".'

There is laughter heard in these years – an ebullience, a delight in the quirky fullness of life, which is not nearly so much in evidence in accounts of his life in Berlin. These were the most public years of his life, and there are friends, colleagues and students on record and ready with a fund of reminiscence and anecdote.

He always wrote out his lectures word for word and read them, but most students apparently never guessed because he gave such a carefully rehearsed performance. His account of the death agonies of Gogol – six fat white blood-letting leeches clinging to his nose – was a legendary set-piece. And one former student, the critic Alfred Appel, has this particularly vivid recollection of Nabokov's gift for spontaneous improvisation in a lecture he gave at Cornell:

It was a cold day, cloudless and silver-skied, the clean hard snow and icicles around Goldwin Smith Hall glinting in the sun. Professor Nabokov, however, was quite dull as he asserted the greatness of Anna Karenina *in an abstract manner uncharacteristic of him [. . .] He was, as they say in show business, losing his audience, bombing in Ithaca [. . .] Nabokov stopped lecturing, abruptly, and, without a word, strode to the right-hand side of the stage and snapped off the three overhead light fixtures. Then he walked down the five or six steps to the floor of*

the lecture hall, clumped up the aisle to the back, two hundred dis-
mayed heads turning together [. . .] to watch him as he silently pulled
down the shades of three or four large windows, curtaining those daz-
zling icicles and darkening the room [. . .] Nabokov retreated down the
aisle, up the stairs, and returned to stage right and the control switch.
'In the firmament of Russian literature', he proclaimed, 'this is
Pushkin!' The ceiling light on the far left of the planetarium went on.
'This is Gogol!' The middle light went on. 'This is Chekhov!' The light
on the right went on. Then Nabokov descended the stage once again,
marched to the rear and the central window, and released the window
shade, which sprang back on its roller (bang!), a solid wide beam of
brilliant sunlight streaming into the room, like some emanation. 'And
that is Tolstoy!' boomed Nabokov.

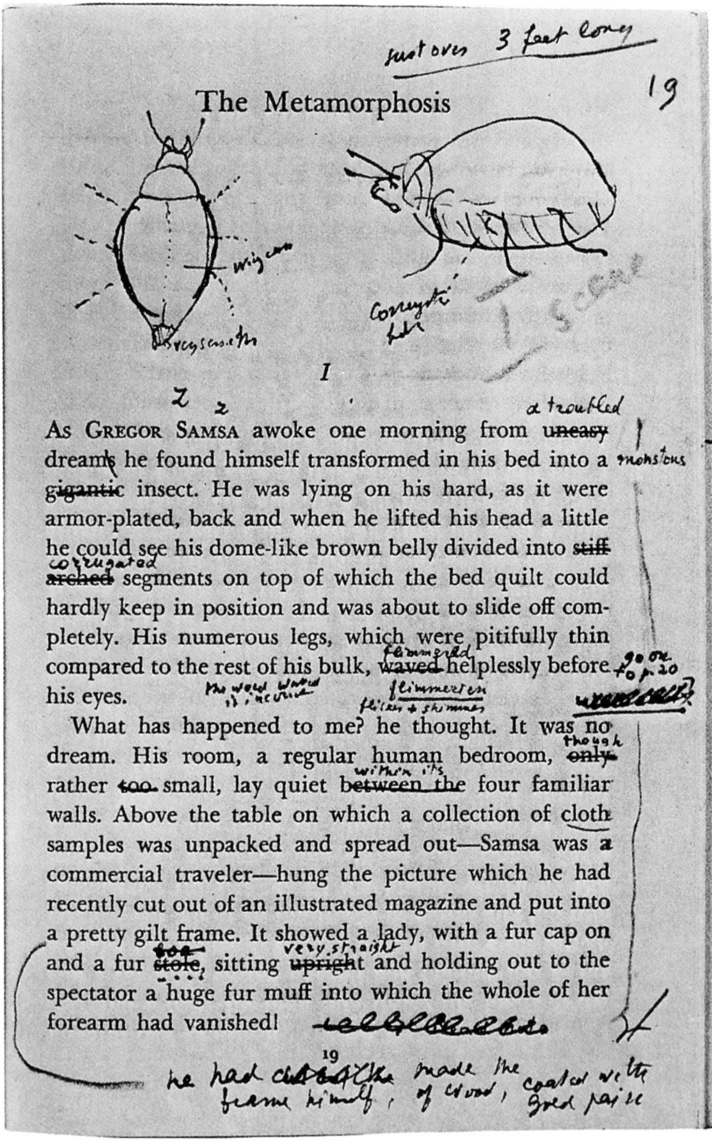

just over 3 feet long

The Metamorphosis

19

wing cases

corrugated tube

SCALE

leg segments

I

Z z

a troubled

As GREGOR SAMSA awoke one morning from ~~uneasy~~
dreams he found himself transformed in his bed into a *monstrous*
~~gigantic~~ insect. He was lying on his hard, as it were
armor-plated, back and when he lifted his head a little
he could see his dome-like brown belly divided into ~~stiff~~
corrugated
~~arched~~ segments on top of which the bed quilt could
hardly keep in position and was about to slide off completely. His numerous legs, which were pitifully thin
flimmered
compared to the rest of his bulk, ~~waved~~ helplessly before *go oz.*
to p. 20
his eyes. *the word waved* *flimmersen*
is incorrect *flicker + shimmer*
~~waved~~

What has happened to me? he thought. It was no ~~dream~~.
though
His room, a regular human bedroom, ~~only~~
within its
rather ~~too~~ small, lay quiet ~~between the~~ four familiar
walls. Above the table on which a collection of cloth
samples was unpacked and spread out—Samsa was a
commercial traveler—hung the picture which he had
recently cut out of an illustrated magazine and put into
a pretty gilt frame. It showed a lady, with a fur cap on
very straight
and a fur ~~stole~~, sitting ~~upright~~ and holding out to the
spectator a huge fur muff into which the whole of her
forearm had vanished!

he had ~~clothed the~~ made the coats of the
frame himself, of wood, 3rd part

He used his drawing skills to make good use of the blackboard – 'grayboard' as he chose to call it. There, ever the meticulous naturalist, he illustrated his point that had Kafka only had a better knowledge of entomology he would have known that poor Gregor Samsa in 'The Metamorphosis' was not trapped in his room, for the beetle he had described was one that could fly. Or he would have the fine-featured white-haired woman he referred to merely as his 'assistant' draw something on the board for him: 'My assistant will now draw an oval-faced woman.' The oval-faced woman was Emma Bovary. The assistant was his wife, Véra, a silent presence at practically all his lectures, an inseparable part of the act.

There was also a cultivated Old-World manner and eccentricity of dress. His teaming of tweed blazer with salmon-pink shirt, blue sweater and yellow tie gave one student cause to wonder whether he dressed in the dark – this in the synaesthete who liked to expatiate on his painterly sensitivity to colour: 'For me the shades, or rather colors of, say, a fox, a ruby, a carrot, a pink rose, a dark cherry, a flushed cheek, are as different as blue is from green or the royal purple of blood from the English sense of violet blue.' And there were the gaffes of the absent-minded professor, as when he walked into the wrong classroom and started reading his lecture to thirty disconcerted students: 'You have just seen the "Coming Attraction" for literature 325,' he announced once he realized his mistake: 'If you are interested you may register next fall.'

Here, however, any resemblance with his character Pnin began and ended. Nabokov was no figure of fun, nor object of pity on the university campus. It was not just the showmanship or unconventionality that made him remembered, or that turned his lectures on European fiction into the most popular option on the Cornell campus, much to the irritation of his academic colleagues with their PhDs (members of the Department of Philistines, Nabokov called them to his students), but because he taught his students how to read. He taught them that great novels were fairy tales, made out of language and detail, story and structure, not general ideas; that a great writer was not a teacher or moralist or social historian, but an enchanter; that

Opposite *The opening page of Kafka's 'The Metamorphosis' from Nabokov's teaching copy.*

From Nabokov's lectures on Anna Karenina. His drawing of a costume of the kind Kitty would have worn when she skated with Lyovin.

a wise reader learns to tell a good book not with his heart, not so much with his brain, but to wait for the 'telltale tingle in his spine'.

He lent his own writer's gift to open his students' eyes and have them see the way ships 'brightened, and shadowed, and changed' in Dickens's description of the harbour at Deal, follow the intersecting routes of Stephen and Leopold Bloom through the streets of Dublin, notice young Kitty in *Anna Karenina* trying to spear a slippery preserved mushroom with her fork as she senses Lyovin's attentions. Yet he could be a bossy demanding pedagogue as well as a spellbinder. He hectored, as well as lectured. There was prejudice and there was pride. There was prejudice, notably, in his persistent denigration of Dostoevsky. After he left Cornell one student asked his successor whether Dostoevsky was Swedish: 'She knew he wasn't a Russian writer because Professor Nabokov had said so so many times, but since he was so gloomy, she thought he might be a Swede.' There was pride in the Golden Treasury of nineteenth-century Russian literature, which he regretted was so little known to American readers and so inadequately translated. This motivated him to write his short book on Gogol, to translate the medieval Russian epic, *The Song of Igor's Campaign*, and, together with his son, Lermontov's *A Hero of Our Time*, but, above all, to undertake the mammoth task of providing a complete critical edition of Pushkin's *Eugene Onegin*: translation, commentary, Russian text – a project that took him five years to write and another seven to see through to publication. 'Russia will never be able to repay all her debts to me,' was how he summed up this achievement in his parting letter to Edmund Wilson in 1959.

Nabokov taught for eighteen years in America, with a couple of

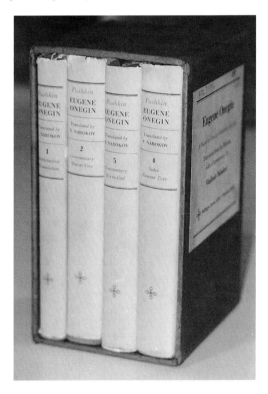

...ugene Onegin. A Novel
...Verse by Aleksandr Pushkin,
...anslated with commentary by
...adimir Nabokov, 4 vols. (New
...rk: Bollingen, 1964).

above *Nabokov and Véra with Dorothy Leuthold, the Russian-language pupil who drove the fam[ily] out to California in June 1941.*
left *Neonympha dorothea. Nabokov's first important America[n] catch, made on the rim of the Grand Canyon, 9 June 1941, and named after Dorothy Leuthold.*

periods of study leave. He put a great deal of time and effort into preparing his lectures, and he clearly derived a measure of satisfaction and modicum of enjoyment from teaching, but he gave it up without regrets. The advantages of easy access to magnificent libraries and long vacations were not offset by the 'ill-paid academic drudgery'. He would repeatedly maintain that a tape-recorder made a more effective tool than the live lecture, and he had little interest in campus life or patience with university politics.

It was quite another matter with his private scholarly pursuits. He never felt the *Eugene Onegin* project to be a burden; rather it acted as a battery-charger, an energizer. He could complain bitterly about the tedium of teaching ('I am sick of teaching, I am sick of teaching, I am sick of teaching'), yet in the very same letter he referred to his work on *Eugene Onegin* as something which 'will not take too much of my time and can be quite smoothly combined with other pleasures'.

Aside from translation, the other inseparable and ever-welcome companion to his teaching years was lepidoptery – the collection and study of butterflies. In the summers the family regularly headed out west. Nabokov made ten trips west in all, two from coast to coast. On the first in June 1941 they were driven from New York to California (destination Stanford where Nabokov had a first appointment teaching creative writing and Russian literature in summer school) by a Russian-language pupil Dorothy Leuthold, and Nabokov caught a new species on the south rim of the Grand Canyon, which he named after her: *Neonympha dorothea*. In 1948 the Nabokovs acquired a car and Véra learned to drive. On all these trips Nabokov pursued his catches, alone or accompanied by Véra, and, albeit with considerably less enthusiasm, by Dmitri. The flying objects the young Dmitri was passionate about were aeroplanes. As Nabokov wrote to his sister Elena, aeroplanes were to Dmitri what butterflies had been to him as a child. As a teenager, though, Dmitri found another way to amuse himself on these trips: rock-climbing. These were the journeys and the motel stops that mapped the America of *Lolita*, while a parent's anxiety at seeing a

Nabokov at work in Harvard's Museum of Comparative Zoology. The inset picture shows Nabokov's drawings of hindwing radial sectors indicating variation in features among related blues from thirteen localities including Yellowstone and Yakima, Washington.

On 15 May 1943 The New Yorker published a poem by Nabokov entitled 'On Discovering a Butterfly'. The first line of the third verse fur-

nished an amusing example of the occasional mistakes Nabokov could make with his English. He originally wrote: 'My needles have teased out its horny sex.' The New Yorker staff pointed out the double entendre; Nabokov amended the offending word to 'sculptured sex', and thanked them for saving him from the 'nightmare pun . . . This has somewhat subdued me – I was getting rather pleased with my English'.

son undertake a life-threatening ascent was to find its way into Nabokov's last story, 'Lance'.

Lepidoptery was not just a summer pursuit. Before he moved to Cornell Nabokov worked for several years, first in a voluntary capacity, then as a part-time research fellow, at the Museum of Comparative Zoology at Harvard. There he worked on the identification and classification of butterflies, specializing in a group of the Lycaenid family of butterflies, known commonly as 'blues'. He was proud of his discoveries, and proud to have butterflies carrying his name, both in their common and their scientific appellations: 'Nabokov's Pug, Nabokov's Blue, Nabokov's Fritillary, Nabokov's Brown, Nabokov's Satyr, Nabokov's Wood Nymph'; '*Lycaeides idas nabokov*', '*Cyllopsis pyracmon nabokovi*'. In the 'ifs' of his personal history he could fantasize on occasion about having become an entomological explorer instead of a writer. This, like the idea of being a landscape painter *manqué*, was a fancy, yet it was an incontrovertible fact that in his scientific work of translation and lepidoptery he found two activities that formed an ideal counterbalance to his writing. As he was fond of saying to his students, with that characteristic Nabokovian twist in the tail of the phrase, the best formula to test the quality of a novel was 'a merging of the precision of poetry and the intuition of science'. And in the early 1940s, when he was still finding his feet in a new world, lepidoptery and translation provided both a safe haven and a valuable linguistic discipline. To Wilson he wrote in 1943 that his scientific writing was providing a 'wonderful bit of training in the use of our (if I may say so) wise, precise, plastic, beautiful English language'. And this is how he described the solace of the laboratory to his sister in 1945: 'To know that an organ you are examining has never been seen by *any one else* before – to plunge into the wonderful crystal world of the microscope, where silence reigns, a silence bounded by its own horizon, a blinding white arena – all this is so fascinating that I cannot begin to describe it.'

Teaching provided the regular source of income and the opportunity to study closely some great books; lepidoptery and translation provided intellectual and emotional ballast, but all were

left *Edmund Wilson and Mary McCarthy, 1941–2.*
below *A sketch by Nabokov of a butterfly,* Papilio bunnyi, *with which he ends an amicable letter to Wilson (3 January 1944): 'I envied Véra immensely when she told me about seeing you. We both wish you and Mary a perfect year. V'.*

'Bunny' was Wilson's pet name, and from as early as 1941 Nabokov and Wilson were addressing each other: 'Dear Bunny'/'Dear Volodya'.

adjuncts to the main mission in coming to America – to become a successful writer of English. He applied himself to this task with the same single-mindedness and unshakeable self-belief as in all his years as Sirin.

But as a virtual unknown in a strange country he needed contacts and an entry into the publishing world, and these were provided by the writer and eminent literary critic Edmund Wilson. The two men became close friends, corresponding regularly, visiting each other's homes, sharing their frustrations and successes, their keen sense of the ridiculous, and their passion for literature. Wilson was married to Mary McCarthy at the time he and Nabokov met, and she too became a great admirer of Nabokov's work, especially later of *Pale Fire*. Within months of meeting Nabokov in 1940 Wilson was arranging for him to do book reviews for the *New*

Republic, and had put him in touch with the literary journal the *Atlantic Monthly*, and with New Directions, which published his first English novel, *The Real Life of Sebastian Knight*, and *Nikolai Gogol*. And it was Wilson who paved the way for Nabokov's most long-standing and profitable collaboration with America's leading literary journal, *The New Yorker*.

It was not all plain sailing, despite the influential contacts. As a Russian Nabokov frequently found himself battling against the tide of political opinion in the war and post-war years. Wellesley did not renew his appointment for a year in 1942, perhaps in part because of his uncompromising antagonism to the Soviet régime, which did not fit in with the new-found sympathy for Russia after Germany invaded. This prompted a wry comment in a letter to Wilson: 'Funny – to know Russian better than any living person – in America at least, – and more English than any Russian in America,

The American writer John Updike in 1960, aged twenty-eight. The young Updike became a mainstay of The New Yorker *in the 1950s and 1960s, and an astute critic and a great admirer of Nabokov's art.*

– and to experience such difficulty in getting a university job.' *The New Yorker* in 1949 also rejected a chapter of his autobiography, finding the denunciation of Lenin too strong. As many of the Third Wave of émigrés were to discover a couple of decades later, a dissident Russian's understanding of liberalism could differ radically from that of a Western democrat. Nabokov's stance on McCarthyism at the end of the 1940s was out of line with American liberal opinion. He could see justification in McCarthy's suspicions of communist infiltration, while wholeheartedly deploring the witch-hunts. Later he was again to find himself in disagreement with his American liberal friends by supporting US government policy over the war in Vietnam.

Politics notwithstanding, after ten years in America Nabokov had an impressive list of publications: stories, poems, the book on Gogol, two novels, *The Real Life of Sebastian Knight* and *Bend Sinister*, and his autobiography. This last was published in America as *Conclusive Evidence* and in England under the title by which it is better known, *Speak, Memory*. He had received some excellent reviews and earned an enviable reputation among the *cognoscenti* of the American East Coast literary world. However, the plain fact was that sales were dismal. In June 1951 he wrote to Wilson: 'I am sick of having my books muffled in silence like gems in cotton wool.' Success was to come only when Nabokov 'took on' America, when he placed the clash of the Old and New Worlds at the centre of his books. This was what he was to do in *Lolita* (1955), *Pnin* (1957) and *Pale Fire* (1962).

Until the mid-1950s there were few of Nabokov's students who knew that Professor Nabokov had once upon a time been a famous writer of Russian, or that, concealed under the obscurity of his own name, he was also a writer of English. Yet Nabokov had made no secret of this. He had no need. All this changed with *Lolita*. From the outset he knew that he had with his story of 'a man who liked little girls' a subject that could get him dismissed from his university post for moral turpitude. He did not mention the project to anyone at Cornell until after the novel had been accepted for publication. For a

First page of the manuscript of the autobiography Conclusive Evidence *(1951), beginning, 'The cradle rocks above the abyss . . .'*

1

The cradle rocks ~~above~~ an abyss, and ~~common~~

~~Our~~ ~~Velvet~~ ~~How~~ ~~tell~~ ~~common~~ assures us that our existence is but a brief
~~crawl~~ strip of light between two eternities of ~~complete~~ darkness. ~~Although~~
~~they~~ although ~~the~~ ~~men may, as a rule,~~
~~that we are~~ (identical twins, ~~but~~ ~~view~~ view
is ~~view~~ by ~~nan~~ a ~~calm~~
the prenatal one ~~with considerably~~ more ~~equanimity~~ equanimity
than the one ~~we are~~ heading for ~~it~~ (at ~~some~~ forty five hundred
heart beats an hour). It is ~~a~~ question of ~~growth~~ and direction of
growth, and ~~to~~ aversion to ~~the~~ growth being stopped ~~was~~ — or
to ~~the my notion~~ of its leading nowhere. ~~Only~~ Now and then, however,
equanimity ~~is~~ given a jolt. ~~I read somewhere~~ of a morbidly
sensitive youth who experienced ~~real~~ panic when looking for
the first time at some ~~home~~ movies that had been ~~taken~~ made
~~youth before~~ a few weeks ~~prior~~ before to his birth. He saw a
world that was practically unchanged — the same house, ~~the~~
same garden, the same people — and then realized that he did
not exist there at all and that nobody mourned his absence.
What particularly frightened him, was the sight of a brand-new
baby carriage ~~t~~ standing there on the porch, with the ~~the~~
~~the smug, encroaching air~~
~~of a coffin~~; even that was empty, as if, his very bones
had ~~already~~ disintegrate.

Such fancies ~~are of course, redolent of youth.~~
~~our early years.~~

Such fancies of that general kind are ~~not~~ strange
to ~~young~~ young lives. ~~Indeed~~ most eschatological
~~sensations~~ often lead to ~~an adolescent~~ ~~—~~ unless
they be directed by some venerable and rigid religion). Nature

See The Conquering Hero Comes—in a Viyella. Robe!

time when he went away he kept it literally under lock and key. When it was finished at the end of 1953 and he began looking for a publisher he was at first adamant that he did not want it to come out under his own name. He foresaw difficulty in getting it published, and *Pnin* was conceived as a work that he could sell as a series of stories to *The New Yorker*, which could tide him over the interim.

In *The Gift* and *The Real Life of Sebastian Knight*, the two novels that he had conceived on the threshold of his new career as a writer of English, he wrote of the risk and the dare of artistic creation. Here was the most challenging feat of 'translation' he ever attempted: to transplant the subject of his abandoned Russian novella *The Enchanter* (*Volshebnik*) on to American soil, to create the immigrant Humbert Humbert and tell the story of his unnatural love for the all-American girl-child Lolita. It was a tale of the capture of a twelve-year-old girl, but also of old Europe's capture and rape of young America. The challenge lay not only in treading a fine line on the borders of art and pornography, high and low literature, but in capturing America of the late 1940s and early 1950s – its language and its culture. He stalked his quarry with all the patience he devoted to the commentary on *Eugene Onegin* and the capture and dissection of butterflies. He assembled the parts of his Lolita with the care of a Dr Coppelius fashioning his life-size doll. He drew up charts on sexual maturation, culled *The American Girl*, *The Best in Teen Tales*, *Calling All Girls*, for teenage fads and fancies, read up on adolescent abnormality and sexual perversion. Edmund Wilson lent him Havelock Ellis's *Etudes de Psychologie Sexuelle* and he 'hugely enjoyed' its 'Sexual Confession of a Russian from the South'. His ear listened out for the idiom and slang of schoolchildren – in the street, from his son, Dmitri, from the daughter of a colleague. His trained artist's eye caught the kitsch that was to become the décor of the Haze home: the Mexican knick-knacks and the 'pinkish cozy, coyly covering the toilet lid'. He entered the dark world of Humbert Humbert's sick mind and showed an enchanted path through the forest leading not to a fairy-tale happy ending as in his remembered childhood bedtime story, but to the sinister enthralment of The Enchanted Hunters motel.

top left *Nabokov's index-card notes used in preparing* Lolita. *Statistics on the height, weight and age of young girls.*

below left *More evidence of Nabokov's background research for* Lolita *and a fine example of his keen eye for the comic potential in American commercialism. Alfred Appel identified this Viyella advertisement as the source for the pin-up which Lolita has on her bedroom wall. 'A full-page ad [. . .] represented a dark-haired young husband with a kind of drained look in his Irish eyes [. . .] modeling a robe by So-and-So and holding a bridgelike tray by So-and-So, with breakfast for two. The legend, by the Rev. Thomas Morell, called him a "conquering hero".' (*Lolita, Part 1, Chapter 16*)

The writing of *Lolita* proved not only a risky undertaking, but also a very demanding one technically, and on more than one occasion Nabokov lost heart and was near to destroying the manuscript, and on more than one occasion Véra dissuaded him and retrieved it from the incinerator. She never, in the five years he spent working on it, from 1948 until the end of 1953, had any doubts about its importance, nor that it should be published. In February 1955, after a year spent vainly trying to interest leading American publishers, Nabokov finally sent it off to an agent in Paris, and when Maurice Girodias of the Olympia Press expressed

an interest, he did not inquire too closely into the publisher's credentials. Indeed, his comment to Wilson after shipping it was that he supposed it might eventually be published 'by some shady firm with a Viennese-Dream name'. He tried to insist that it did not come out under his own name, but when anonymity was denied he signed a contract in June and the book that was to change his life came out in Paris that September. Girodias knew a good book when he saw one, and he was very impressed by the literary quality of *Lolita*, but the Olympia Press was designed as a money-spinner to bring out books that had been rejected by Anglo-American censorship, and Girodias deliberately elected to be indiscriminate, as he explained to *Playboy*. Initially, the publication was received in silence. The Olympia Press did not get reviewed or advertised in the normal way. But then Graham Greene named *Lolita* as one of the three best books of 1955 in the London *Sunday Times* and things happened fast. Gallimard signed up for a French translation. American publishers began making approaches. Controversy, the attempted banning of the book in France, threats of legal action, all made it a hot

below *Cover of the first edition of* Pnin *(Garden City New York: Doubleday, 1957). Nabokov thought it 'a splendid idea' that Pnin should be holding a book on the cover, and suggested (letter, 1 October 1956 to Jacob Epstein) that it should read 'Pnin by V. Nabokov' in cyrillic script.*

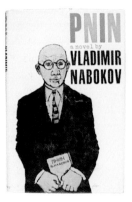

property. Illegal copies were soon on sale in the shops of Ithaca and circulated on campus and Professor Nabokov suddenly found himself something of a cult figure among Cornell's bright young things, among them Thomas Pynchon. *Lolita*'s reputation abroad ensured the immediate success of *Pnin*, which came out in book form in 1957 over a year before *Lolita* itself was finally published in America by Putnam's in 1958. By the end of September of that year *Lolita* stood at the top of the best-seller lists. By December the paperback rights were sold, Nabokov had signed a movie contract with James Harris and Stanley Kubrick, and Groucho Marx knew he could get a laugh with the joke: 'I've put off reading *Lolita* for six years, till she's eighteen.' From genteel obscurity Nabokov was catapulted into a round of public engagements which played havoc with his teaching schedule. He took a year's leave of absence from Cornell and in September 1959 sailed for Europe. Here, after a gap of over twenty years, he was finally reunited with his sister Elena and brother Kirill; here he saw his son Dmitri installed in a new career as an opera singer in Italy, and attended glitzy literary receptions in Paris, London and Milan.

Nabokov was never again to reside permanently in the United States. He resigned from Cornell, returned in 1960 for a few months to Beverly Hills, California, to write the screenplay for *Lolita* (there attending a party where his years as a film-goer rather let him down when he asked John Wayne what he did for a living; 'I'm in pictures,' Wayne replied), then sailed back to Europe. By autumn 1961 he and Véra were installed in the Hotel Montreux Palace, which was to be their home for the rest of his life, and Véra's until 1990, a year before her death.

He left on the crest of a wave. He had built anew, as a writer of English, the career and the reputation he had had as a writer of Russian, he had turned the hard-luck story of the dispossessed

above *880 Highland Road, Cayuga Heights, Ithaca, New York, the house of Lauriston and Ruth Sharp, which the Nabokovs rented for a year from February 1957, looking after their cat, Bandit. Nabokov drew on this setting for John Shade's home in* Pale Fire. *In the words of his biographer Brian Boyd: 'Cat-minding, window, waxwings, shag-bark, swine, horse-shoes – everything about the place was kindling for* Pale Fire.*'*

right *Sue Lyon as Lolita in one of the opening scenes of Stanley Kubrick's film (1962).*

aristocrat into an American dream. While truly amazed at the speed of the roller-coaster ride, he felt it no more than his due. As he wrote to his sister: 'Lolita is a tremendous success – but this all should have happened thirty years ago.' He had made a success not only of Lolita but also of America. Despite never having purchased a property, he had made himself more at home there than anywhere else apart from Russia. He had become an American citizen and a full university professor, he had seen his son through school, through Harvard, and through his military service, had watched him do all-American things: debating, athletics, tennis, dating girls, driving fast cars. And if he had not been too popular with all his faculty colleagues he had made a lasting impression on generations of students. He had also carved himself a memorable place in the history of *The New Yorker*. He had loved the sheer size and the wealth of natural beauty of America. It reminded him in some respects of Russia, as did the warmth and openness of its people, an openness that he had not encountered among the English or the Germans. He felt at ease. And if he found American life just as rich a source of philistinism (in Russian, *poshlost'*, or *poshlust*, as he punned it) as Germany, yet here he saw no evil, and instead of being disgusted he laughed. However, behind the banter and American *bonhomie* he remained a man apart. He used humour not just to 'connect', to borrow an American expression, but also to keep his distance. Although his life in America was more public than ever before or after, he and Véra remained essentially private people. Looking back, more than one friend might have wondered whether they had ever known him well. Yet the essential job was done: Nabokov's works had reached their reader. John Updike spoke for many when he said: 'he is now an American writer and the best living'.

Return to Europe: 1959–1977

MONTREUX

They are passing, posthaste, posthaste, the gliding years ...
(*Speak, Memory*, Chapter 15)

Nabokov was sixty when he left America. He planned to return for good, and spoke often of doing so, but as time went by the idea faded until it was little more than a dream. In the Montreux Palace Hotel where he and Véra settled in October 1961 he had ideal living and working conditions, right in the centre of town, yet secluded from the public eye, with Véra at his side, his sister only an hour away in Geneva, his son just across the border in Italy, and good butterflies up on the Alpine slopes. Dmitri was pursuing his career as an opera singer, as well as doing some car racing, but was on hand to play a vital part in the task to which Nabokov dedicated a major part of his last years – the translation of the main body of his Russian writing into English. A reader can sense the glow of pride in his Foreword to the last of the translated novels, *Glory* (1971): 'The present work closes the series of definitive English versions in which my entire set of nine Russian novels [...] is available to American and British readers.' Nabokov had never put undue pressure on Dmitri to do anything other than follow his own lights in a choice of career, yet he had always encouraged him to take up translation and entertained the hope that he would some day become his translator. He was ultimately to be amply rewarded not only by the commitment Dmitri showed, but also by his abundant talent. Dmitri made translations of most of the drama, the stories and six of the nine novels.

Nabokov's sister Elena also found herself co-opted into the family firm, once she began making regular return visits to Leningrad after 1969. While

Always the writer. Nabokov on a bench in the garden of the Montreux Palace Hotel using a box of index cards as an improvised desk.

Nabokov remained unshakeable in his resolve never to set foot in the Soviet Union, he made good use of Elena as his spy, his *soglia-datai*, when he came to imagine the return to Russia of his fictional *alter ego* Vadim Vadimych N. in his last novel, *Look at the Harlequins!* In Elena he found he had not only a keen eye but also someone who shared his precious store of childhood memories of Russia. They had corresponded since 1945 when she was still in Prague, comparing notes on their two growing sons, on their jobs, on books (she was an excellent reader of his work) and, most importantly, on the past. She could tell her brother that for twenty-three years she had had exactly the same dream of their father as he had described in *The Gift*. He could write to his sister in the winter of 1946 that a piece of his father's blue-and-white striped dressing-gown was hung at his bathroom window to keep out the

draught. And to her he could write of his horror at the news of Sergey's fate and of his loathing for the Germans, with their concentration camps and their killing of children. In the late 1940s he had tapped into his sister's memory bank and been a more assiduous correspondent when he was first gathering material for his autobiography. He was to do so again for the revised version, *Speak, Memory: An Autobiography Revisited*, in the 1960s.

Thus there were practical reasons for staying put in Montreux. But the location also fed his artistic imagination in this last period of his life and matched his growing sense of finally being rid of any exclusive linguistic or national label or tie and able to travel freely in space-time. In Montreux he could hear French, German, English and Italian spoken daily in the hotel lobby. He could stroll out to the news-stand in the Grand Rue and find newspapers on sale in a dozen languages. He enjoyed the awareness that Russian writers of the past century had been travellers in the area – Zhukovsky, Gogol, Dostoevsky, Tolstoy – and other writers too: Rousseau, Byron, Daudet. In the stylish luxury of the old Swan wing he could feel the time warp and slip back to the European trips of his childhood, and home to pre-Revolutionary St Petersburg with its household of servants. Yet in his hotel rooms in July 1969 he could rent a television set and gaze entranced at the 'gentle little minuet' danced by the two first Americans on the moon. For years he had been enchanted by the romance of space travel. Between 1959 and 1966 he had toyed with plots combining that romance with an interplanetary love story, and in 1964 had responded to a request from Alfred Hitchcock with a brief synopsis of the love of an astronaut and a starlet. No film came out of this. Instead, Nabokov wrote *Ada* (original working title *Letters from Terra*), published in May 1969, his longest, most ambitious, most demanding novel, the distilled product of his fascination with space-time, and much more besides.

Once the moon-landing was over, the rented television was promptly returned, but Nabokov continued to ponder the coming together of time past, time present and time yet to come, and the patterning of his life blending with the pattern of art. From his

irst men on the moon, 20 July
969.
In his story 'Lance' (1952) Nabokov
ad made it clear that it was not the
ocket racket' that excited his imagi-
ation, not the 'frenzy of compet-
ive confusion, phony gravitation,
nd savagely flappy flags'. On 3 July
969 he cabled this reply to Thomas
amilton for publication in The
ew York Times, with, he points
ut, 'a disastrous misprint in the
eventh word': 'TREADING THE SOIL
F THE MOON PALPATING ITS
EBBLES TASTING THE PANIC AND
PLENDOR OF THE EVENT FEELING
N THE PIT OF ONES STOMACH THE
EPARATION FROM TERRA THESE
ORM THE MOST ROMANTIC SEN-
ATION AN EXPLORER HAS EVER
NOWN.' *(Strong Opinions,* Letter
973)

balcony window he could look out on the same lake and the same
swan that he had seen forty years ago when he visited his old governess Cécile Miauton, whom he had made into 'Mademoiselle O'.
He knew that his apartments on the sixth floor into which he and
Véra had removed in September 1962 (less spacious than their
third-floor rooms, but much quieter, and complete with attic
library) had been vacated by the nephew of a one-time family
acquaintance, the artist Alexander Benois. Benois had been a vis-
itor to the St Petersburg house, and his paintings had once hung
in its rooms. Yet Benois's nephew was no ghost from the past. He
was the actor and writer Peter Ustinov, fresh from making *Spartacus*
with the man who was now directing *Lolita* – Stanley Kubrick. The

J. J. 7844 *Clarens. Ile des Mouettes.*

Lake Geneva with its swans, 1912.
Photo of L'Ile des mouettes (now Il
de Salagnon), Clarens, Montreux.

Ustinovs moved out of Montreux and built a chalet up in the mountains in nearby Les Diablerets. The Nabokovs followed their lead and bought a plot of land there, but they never built on it, and never moved.

Nabokov's growing awareness of the interweave of time and place, life and art left its mark on his Montreux writing. In his revision of *Speak, Memory* he continually linked the present with the recent and the distant past. He brought people to life with echoes of fiction: evoking the village schoolmaster through Tolstoy, and his Uncle Rukavishnikov with a nod to the character of Arkady's uncle, Pavel Petrovich Kirsanov, in Turgenev's *Fathers and Sons*. He planned to write a sequel and call it *Speak On, Memory*. He never did, just as he planned to go back to live in America but never did, or rather he did, but (like Gogol when he wrote *Dead Souls* 'from his beautiful distance' of Western Europe) in fiction, not in fact, in the imaginary worlds he created in *Ada*, *Transparent Things* and *Look at the Harlequins!*

The writer Herbert Gold recalled Nabokov saying once, 'I travel through life in a space helmet,' and saw it as an apt metaphor for his insulation and isolation and the overview of the universe that he had. Like a space traveller, he could sometimes get out of the space helmet, but he saw the universe from its protection. In the Montreux years fewer and fewer people saw Nabokov without his helmet. The public image he projected in interviews and in the Forewords to his translated novels was studiedly aloof and remote. There was wit and humour and fine feeling, but a rebarbative arrogance. There was a hardening of the emotional arteries, the strong opinions became stronger and positions more entrenched. Some observers detected a hypersensitivity to slights (especially to slights against his wife), and an interest in settling old scores, which might have been forgivable in an insecure young writer but seemed less than befitting to someone who was so pre-eminently successful. The Russian version of his autobiography, *Drugie berega* (*Other Shores*, 1954), had already given offence in émigré quarters for its cool appraisal of Bunin, who had died the year before. Nabokov added in this version a poignant pastiche of the falling cadences of Bunin's prose. But he did not omit or modify his recollection of Bunin prophesying that he, Nabokov, would die in dreadful pain and complete isolation, this when Bunin's last years had been spent in illness and severely straitened circumstances. Certain of Nabokov's old émigré acquaintances, especially those who harboured anti-Semitic feelings, judged that Véra was to blame. She had always managed the practical side of Nabokov's life. Now some felt she had taken over, and controlled him. A number of old friends had reason to feel slighted and forgotten, and deplored the transformation of their handsome, fine-boned Sirin, master of Russian style, into the heavy-jowled American who stared out of the cover of *Time* and *Newsweek*, author of that vulgar piece of popular fiction, *Lolita*. With *Lolita* they felt Nabokov had let the side down.

It did not help Nabokov's reputation with some fellow Russians that *Lolita* had appeared at the same time as Pasternak's *Doctor Zhivago*. Here were two novels that had both had a difficult publishing history: *Zhivago* had been refused publication in the Soviet Union by the journal *Novyi mir* (*New World*), while *Lolita* had been initially rejected by five American publishers. Yet how different they

FIFTY CENTS

MAY 23, 1969

TIME

THE NOVEL IS ALIVE
and Living in Antiterra

VLADIMIR
NABOKOV

opposite Time *cover illustration on the occasion of* Ada's *publication, May 1969.*

right *Boris Pasternak toasting the news that he had been awarded the Nobel Prize for Literature, with Nina Tabidze (left) and his wife, Zinaida Nikolaevna, at home in his dacha at Peredelkino, 23 November 1958. Pasternak was subsequently pressurized by the Soviet authorities into refusing the award.*

were. While Pasternak was seen to have spoken out boldly against the evils of the Soviet régime under Stalin and was in consequence hounded by the Soviet authorities, labelled an internal émigré and compelled to forgo the Nobel Prize, Nabokov was seen by his detractors to have sold out for a quick buck. Nor did it help that Nabokov was so damning about *Zhivago*. In public he was content to call it trashy, melodramatic, false and inept. In private he also condemned its politics, calling it Sovietophile and completely anti-liberal. From someone who had been dislodged by Pasternak from the No. 1 slot on the best-seller list, and who had failed himself to win the Nobel Prize, this looked like a bad case of sour grapes.

In the acutely politicized world of the Russian emigration Nabokov still, as he had done in the interwar years, cut a lone figure. As the Third Wave of émigré dissidents reached the West in the 1960s and 1970s Russia-watchers on both sides of the Atlantic and the Iron Curtain were keen to see Nabokov come forward as a human rights champion. Many were disappointed. Nabokov did speak out on occasion, but only rarely. He made a public protest in the *Observer* against the imprisonment of the young writer Vladimir Bukovsky in a Soviet psychiatric hospital. He received the newly arrived Soviet writers Victor Nekrasov and Vladimir Maksimov; and he laid on a private lunch for Solzhenitsyn in the Montreux Palace when he was in Switzerland in 1974. It was due to a pure misunderstanding that the two men missed each other on that occasion, yet no rematch was arranged. Nabokov had enormous sympathy for the human rights movement and

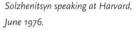

Solzhenitsyn speaking at Harvard, June 1976.

respect for Soviet writers' courage in fighting for freedom of expression, yet he and they spoke different languages. Polemic, political satire, bare truth-telling – these were not his weapons or his themes.

Another bone of contention for Russians who read English was the damage Nabokov had done to their greatest poet in his *Eugene Onegin*. The shackling of Pushkin's limpid masterpiece to three volumes of self-indulgent commentary was viewed by some as an outrageous act of hubris, while the pedantry and awkwardness of the literal English translation prompted the émigré Harvard economist Alexander Gerschenkron to wonder whether this was a bad case of anxiety of influence and describe it in an influential review article as 'a labor of love and a work of hate'.

Pushkin was certainly not the revered cultural icon to Western readers that he was to Russians. Indeed, there would have been quite a number of Westerners hard-pressed to say who he was. Yet it was this work of scholarly exegesis that occasioned one of the most protracted and public literary quarrels of the 1960s and early 1970s – between Nabokov and Edmund Wilson. It was conducted on both sides of the Atlantic in the pages of *The New York Review of Books*, *The New York Times Book Review*, *Encounter*, the *New Statesman*, as well as in Wilson's memoir *Upstate* and his posthumously published collection of essays, *A Window on Russia*. It made for a sorry and undignified end to a long-standing, genuinely warm friendship from which both men had derived benefit.

There had always been a competitive edge to the relationship, an element of teasing one-upmanship (what Wilson called 'intellectual romps, sometimes accompanied by mauling'), and they had argued strongly about politics and literature, *Zhivago* being a notable subject of difference, but as long as Nabokov remained in America the bond of friendship had held. Yet it did not withstand the change in Nabokov's fortunes after *Lolita* – the sudden translation of the destitute immigrant protégé into an international celebrity. Nabokov was deeply hurt by the personal nature of Wilson's attack and hit back hard, yet was too fastidious to air in print that it was envy he saw as the cause. It was ironic that the first

and only project on which the two men had collaborated was a translation of Pushkin's tale of artistic rivalry, *Mozart and Salieri* – a collaboration that had elicited these words of praise to Wilson from Nabokov in 1941: 'It is quite perfect now – you have played your Mozart to my Salieri.'

If Nabokov came off marginally the moral victor in this bitter polemic, still there is sympathy for the loser. For might not Wilson's resentment have been fuelled by the suspicion that he had been used, and had unwittingly helped create Nabokov's greatest success, *Lolita*? Had Nabokov merely been foraging for material when he showed such an interest in elegant pornography, exchanged *risqué* books, sexual innuendo and sophisticated 'dirty talk'? Was there a sly dig at Wilson's pet theory that artistic creativity springs from trauma (set out in his well-known essay 'The Wound and the Bow') when Humbert Humbert attributes his nymphomania to a lost childhood love, and writes that 'the poison was in the wound, and the wound remained ever open'? Was all of life for Nabokov, including this

'Lolita and the Two Bears', New Statesman, *19 October 1979. Cartoon by Richard Willson accompanying John Bayley's review of* The Nabokov–Wilson Letters, 1940–1971, *ed. S. Karlinsky. Willson's drawing wittily picks out two well-chewed bones of contention: Edmund Wilson is seen putting his critical pencil to work on a page of* Eugene Onegin, *while Nabokov disdainfully holds unopened a book by Jane Austen.*

friendship, merely a means, to quote the Decadent Russian poet Bryusov, 'to make brightly singing verses'?

Wilson might have wondered whether he played any part in the creation of *Lolita*, but might not Andrew Field, Nabokov's first biographer, have also wondered what he contributed to the making of *Look at the Harlequins!*? Nabokov had seen merit in Field's first book about him, and concurred when Field volunteered 'to be his Boswell'. He gave time and encouragement to the project. Yet he was appalled by the result. When he saw a draft in 1973 he wrote to Field saying he 'would attribute to the workings of a deranged mind some of its wild rubbish', and broke off relations. But he then went straight to work on the last rewrite of his novel – a travesty of an autobiography by an insane writer. Nabokov had already created memorable parodies of biography in *The Gift* and *The Real Life of Sebastian Knight*. Field must have known well Nabokov's creative pattern of art to life to art; after all, he had entitled his first book *Nabokov: A Life in Art*. Might he not have anticipated his fate and guessed that he might be sucked into the artist's mirror when he overheard Nabokov say to his wife after he had taken his leave one evening: 'Darling, can I really not write about him?' This followed by: 'Oh, I'm terribly sorry, Andrew. I didn't realize you *were* still here'?

The Wilson and Field disputes were unpleasant episodes that darkened Nabokov's last years. Yet there was a lot of light and good humour. Behind the cultivated aloofness Nabokov was in chosen company sociable and fun. And though he recoiled in distaste at the vulgarization of the Lolita image, he enjoyed the fame, the interviews and the photoshoots, and – as long as he could still feel himself in control – his notoriety. Not that his life in Montreux was the lotus-eating existence it sometimes amused him to portray. There was a discipline and dedication to the task of putting his life's work in order – supervising the translations and writing the last novels. While this main task was virtually accomplished, some projects had to be regretfully abandoned or were not completed. One of these was to make a complete catalogue of the *Butterflies of Europe*; another was a planned scientific study of butterflies in painting,

Butterflies in Art. In his last years he did not have
quite the energy and the phenomenal capacity for
work that he had shown in his youth and middle
years, but he followed a regular daily working routine. The regular pattern of his days was matched
by the regular pattern of his year. There was a
return to the hiemal–aestival pattern of his childhood and the best of his American years: winters
writing in town, summers spent travelling and
hunting butterflies. Only in early summer 1976 was
the pattern interrupted when he tripped and fell on
the bathroom floor, suffered concussion, and was
ten days in hospital. Thereafter he had bouts of illness and further stays in hospital and could write
little. He died of fluid build-up in the lungs in
Lausanne hospital on 2 July the following year,
leaving one last novel, *The Original of Laura*, unfinished.

Nabokov liked to make out that he had led a fairly uneventful
life. He said that it resembled a bibliography rather than a biography, and that 'the best part of a writer's biography is not the
record of his adventures but the story of his style'. He was wrong
about his life being dull. Not so. It was a life packed with incident
and drama, a tale of lucky escapes and blind cruel tragedy, dispos-
session and recovery, a life shaped by the forces that have shaped

To Véra

Arlequinus arlequinus

opposite *Nabokov on La
Videmanette (2,220 m) above
Rougemont near Gstaad, August
1971, on a walk with Dmitri. That
day Nabokov told Dmitri 'that he
had accomplished what he wished in
life and art, and was a truly happy
man'.*

above *A last butterfly for Véra,
Arlequinus arlequinus. A male
butterfly, drawn for Véra in
Montreux, August 1974, in a copy of
Look at the Harlequins!, his last
completed novel.*

our times – war, Revolution, Communism and Fascism. A very paradigm of the twentieth century. His novels and stories are fashioned out of its fractures and dark materials. Yet they bear little trace of the cynicism, pessimism and disillusionment that dominate other writers' response to those years, nor do they engage in the business of passing judgement or setting the world to rights. Nabokov 'engaged' all right, but he engaged with natural beauty, with human closeness and love, with humour and with joy, as well as with the mysteries beyond our understanding, and he did it in the best and only way he knew how – by writing in an extraordinary way. He needed no other epitaph on his headstone: he was 'a writer'.

below *Nabokov's gravestone at Clarens, just outside Montreux. Today the headstone also bears Véra's name.*

opposite *The Rukavishnikov mansion at Rozhdestveno, currently being restored after the fire of 1995.*

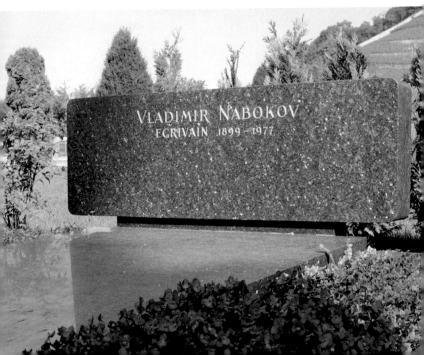

VLADIMIR NABOKOV
ÉCRIVAIN 1899 – 1977

The End

The writer's art is his real passport.

(*Strong Opinions*, Interview 1966)

Time and the tape run on. Nearly twenty-five years have gone by. 'Nymphet', the word Nabokov coined, has entered the *OED*, while 'Lolita' has been writ large over the door of a good many less reputable establishments. In Nabokov's house there are indeed many mansions and workmen have been busy in well nigh all of them. In Russia the *perestroik*-ers have put up scaffolding everywhere – in the place of his christening, inside and outside the Tenishev School. The ground floor of the town house is now a Nabokov Museum, splendidly refurbished; and that too is the intention for

German graffito on the wall of one of the upstairs rooms of the Rozhdestveno mansion. This vivid reminder of the German occupation during the Second World War was destroyed in the 1995 fire. The verse inscription reads:

> If he doesn't have beer,
> If he doesn't have wine,
> Then in the meantime,
> A Schnapps would be fine.

the imposing manor at Rozhdestveno once it has been re-restored (for it burned down in 1995), in full view of the spanking bright brick villas of the 'new Russians' that are ribboning along the river bank. Memorialists have been busy with the unveiling of statues and the laying on of plaques, while archivists have been searching out the lost property (the confiscated artworks, the family books) and putting traces on the missing persons. Scientists have been evaluating Nabokov's standing in the field of lepidoptery, while academics on their ever higher chairs dissect the gossamer filaments of his art. Nabokov's wife Véra died in 1991 and her ashes are now interred with his at Clarens. Their son, Dmitri, at Montreux in his residence overlooking the Palace Hotel and the lake, loyally, expertly and with great love sees to the affairs of the estate and completes unfinished business.

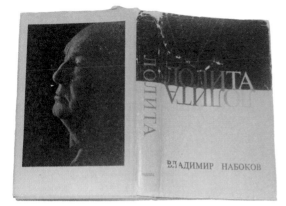

First Russian edition of Lolita *in Nabokov's own translation (New York: Phaedra, 1967). Nabokov took care over his cover designs. Note the rainbow lettering of the dust cover and the sugar-pink binding – a far cry from the dingy colourings of most Soviet-published books.*

Many cracks in the image have now been plastered over and gaps in the life filled. A former tutor has supplied an ending for the young school chum Kolya Shustov (nameless in the autobiography) whom Nabokov so guiltily remembers abandoning to go off catching butterflies: he died working as a nurse in the Civil War. The daughter of Nabokov's long-lost first love, Liussya, has come forward (meet Natalya Mitrofanovna Styopina) to tell her story and the story of her mother. Biographers are putting the spotlight on other characters, and adopting new camera angles. Welcome new light and fresh footprints, but care must be taken lest they overlay the pattern of Nabokov's own telling, fill its silences and and take away its shade.

Ghosts still walk, though. Nothing magical or mystical, just shadows of sense echoed in the perception of Nabokov's readers. Here a key line from *Pale Fire* overheard by a keen amateur of Nabokov's metaphysics: 'No, no dear. Not "mountain". "Fountain",' says a young mother to her young child in his pushchair, as they pause in front of the huge stone fountain in Trinity College, Cambridge's Great Court. Here, for the reader who savours Nabokov's sense of the ridiculous, a chance reincarnation of 'Mademoiselle O' by the shores of Lake Geneva in the guise of a clumsy metal waste bin bearing the label MIAUTON. Here, for the sentimentalist, the clear voice of an erect grey-bunned woman calling out 'Lo-li-ta! Lo-li-ta!' to her elderly friend across the long grass in the Tauride Palace Gardens in St Petersburg, where young Nabokov once walked with his Liussya.

But these are the ghosts of Nabokov's creations and the creations of his readers, not Nabokov. Nabokov is at rest. He always said that he would return to Russia in his books. Now he has. He translated *Lolita* himself into Russian, and Véra made a Russian translation of *Pale Fire* after he died. Finally, now, all his books have returned there and his writer's migration cycle is completed. He has at last reached not just his European and Anglo-American readers, but *all* his readers. He can disappear into his books, not with the grin of Alice's Cheshire Cat, but with a typographical smile.

Question: *How do you rank yourself among writers (living) and of the immediate past?*
Answer: *I often think there should exist a special typographical sign for a smile – some sort of concave mark, a supine round bracket, which I would now like to trace in reply to your question.*
(Strong Opinions, Interview 1969)

Chronology

From 1800 to 1918 Russia followed the Julian calendar, which up until 1 January 1900 was twelve days behind the Western or Gregorian (New Style) calendar, and, from 1900, thirteen days behind. Thus Nabokov's date of birth was 10 April 1899 in St Petersburg and 22 April (New Style) in Western Europe, but after 1900 its anniversary became 23 April, thereby coinciding, as Nabokov himself liked to point out, with Shakespeare's birthday.

1899   *10/22 April*: Birth in St Petersburg, Russia, of Vladimir Vladimirovich, first child of Vladimir Dmitrievich Nabokov and Elena Ivanovna Nabokov.

1900   *February 28/March 13*: Birth of brother Sergey.

1902   *24 December/5 January 1903*: Birth of sister Olga.

1904   *6–9/19–22 November*: First national congress of *zemstvos* held in St Petersburg. Final session held in Nabokov home.

1905   *9/22 January*: 'Bloody Sunday'. Tsar's troops fire at demonstration of workers converging on the Winter Palace.
       October: General strike in Russia.

1906   *March*: Birth of sister Elena (18/31); V. D. Nabokov elected as Kadet candidate for First State Duma.
       10/23 July: V. D. Nabokov barred from politics for signing Vyborg manifesto opposing conscription and taxes.

1908   *May–August*: V. D. Nabokov serves three-month sentence in Kresty Prison.

1911   *January*: Vladimir and Sergey enrolled at Tenishev School.
       June: Birth of brother Kirill.

1914   First poems.
       War declared.

1915   Beginning of first love affair, with Valentina ('Liussya') Shulgina.

1916   *June*: *Stikhi* (*Poems*) privately printed in Petrograd.
       Autumn: Death of 'Uncle Ruka' (Vasily Rukavishnikov) who bequeathed his estate in Russia (Rozhdestveno) and a substantial fortune to his nephew.

1917   *27 February/12 March*: February Revolution. V. D. Nabokov holds office in the provisional government.
       24–5 October/6–7 November: October Revolution/Bolshevik coup.

V. D. Nabokov sends family to Crimea (November) and succeeds in joining them in the south.

1919   *March/April*: Collapse of anti-Bolshevik resistance in the Crimea.
        2/15 April: Nabokov family sails from Sebastopol for Athens.
        27 May: Nabokov family arrives in London.

1919–22 Vladimir Nabokov at Trinity College, Cambridge.
        August 1920: V. D. Nabokov moves family to Berlin and begins editing newspaper *Rul'* (*The Rudder*).

1922   *28 March*: V. D. Nabokov killed at a public meeting.
        June: Vladimir Nabokov graduates from Cambridge and becomes engaged to Svetlana Siewert in Berlin.
        Summer: Translates *Alice in Wonderland* into Russian (published 1923).
        December: *Grozd'* (*The Cluster*) published, mostly poems for Svetlana Siewert.

1923   *January*: Engagement to Svetlana Siewert broken off.
        Publication of poetry collection *Gornii put'* (*Empyrean Path*).
        May: Meets Véra Evseevna Slonim.
        October: Mother moves to Prague.

1924   Begins several years of tutoring (English, Russian, tennis, boxing). Writes stories and composes with Ivan Lukash sketches for Russian cabarets in Berlin.

1925   *15 April*: Marries Véra Slonim in Berlin town hall.

1926   First novel, *Mary*, published.

1928   Second novel, *King, Queen, Knave*, written and published.

1929   Serialized publication of *The Defense* in *Sovremennye zapiski* (*Contemporary Annals*). Publication of collection of stories and poems, *The Return of Chorb*.

1930   Completed serialization of *The Defense*, published in book form later in the year. The novella, *The Eye*, published in *Sovremennye zapiski*. Writes *Glory* (published 1931).

1931   Writes *Camera Obscura* (published 1932–3).

1932   Writes *Despair* (published 1934).

1933   Begins work on *The Gift*.
        Hitler comes to power.
        Ivan Bunin awarded the Nobel Prize for Literature.

1934   *10 May*: Birth of son, Dmitri.
        Breaks off *The Gift* to write *Invitation to a Beheading* (published 1935–6).

1935   Makes his own English translation of *Despair*.

1936   *January*: Writes 'Mademoiselle O' in French.
          January–February: Reading tour of Brussels, Antwerp, Paris.
          May: Véra loses her last German job and Nabokov begins seeking
          employment in the English-speaking world.

1937   *January*: Leaves Germany.
          February: Begins affair with Irina Guadanini.
          May: Joins Véra and Dmitri in Prague.
          July: Moves with family to Cannes.
          September: Retranslates, rewrites and retitles *Camera Obscura* as
          Laughter in the Dark.
          Last meeting with Irina.

1938   *January*: Completes *The Gift* (published serially 1937–8, minus the
          Chernyshevsky chapter).
          December: Writing first English novel, *The Real Life of Sebastian
          Knight* (finished January 1939).

1939   *May*: Death of mother in Prague.
          October–November: Writes novella *The Enchanter*, first attempt at
          the *Lolita* story.

1940   *May*: Nabokovs sail from France to the US.
          October: Meets Edmund Wilson.

1941   *May*: Offered one-year appointment in comparative literature,
          Wellesley College.
          June: Driven with family across US to California.
          June–August: Teaches creative writing and Russian literature at
          Stanford.
          December: Publication of *The Real Life of Sebastian Knight*.

1942   *June*: Appointed Research Fellow in Entomology at the Museum of
          Comparative Zoology, Harvard.

1944   *August*: *Nikolai Gogol* published.
          September: Appointed lecturer at Wellesley College.

1945   *July*: Nabokovs become US citizens.
          Hears of death of brother Sergey in Nazi concentration camp.

1947   *April*: Begins planning *Lolita* and autobiography.
          June: Publication of *Bend Sinister*.
          December: Publication of *Nine Stories*.

1948   *July*: Takes up appointment as Professor of Russian Literature,
          Cornell University.

1950   *April*: In hospital with neuralgia intercostalis.
          Summer: Begins writing *Lolita*. Dissatisfied, nearly burns manu-
          script.

1951 *February*: Publication of autobiography, *Conclusive Evidence*.
      September: Dmitri starts Harvard BA.
1952 *Spring*: Visiting lecturer at Harvard.
      April: Russian original of *The Gift* published in book form, com-
      plete with the missing Chernyshevsky chapter.
1953 On leave from Cornell.
      December: Finishes *Lolita*.
1954 Work on *Pnin* and *Eugene Onegin*. Publication of Russian version of
      autobiography, *Drugie berega* (*Other Shores*).
1955 *August*: *Pnin* completed (published 1957).
      September: *Lolita* published in Paris.
1957 *December*: Completes edition of *Eugene Onegin* (published 1964).
1958 *August*: *Lolita* published in US.
1959 *January*: Delivers last Cornell lecture.
      February: Finishes translation of *Song of Igor's Campaign* (pub-
      lished 1960).
      September: *Invitation to a Beheading* published in English.
      Sails to Europe.
1960 *Spring–early summer*: Writes *Lolita* screenplay for Stanley Kubrick in
      California.
      November: Begins *Pale Fire*.
1961 *October*: Moves to the Palace Hotel, Montreux.
      December: Completes *Pale Fire* (published 1962).
1962 *June*: Attends première of Kubrick's *Lolita* in New York.
1963 *May*: English version of *The Gift* published.
1964 *January*: Edmund Wilson visits for the last time.
      April: Brother Kirill dies of a heart attack in Munich.
      September: English version of *The Defense* published.
1965 *March*: Completes Russian translation of *Lolita* (published 1967).
      15 July: Publication of Edmund Wilson's hostile review of *Eugene
      Onegin* in *The New York Review of Books*, sparking a sharp exchange
      of views extending into 1966.
      September: Cancels long-standing project on *Butterflies of Europe*.
      English version of *The Eye* published.
      November: Begins revising *Speak, Memory* (published January
      1967).
1966 *May*: Nabokov's second revised English version of *Despair* pub-
      lished.
1968 *April*: Revised English translation of *King, Queen, Knave* published.
      October: Completes *Ada* (begun early 1966).

1969	*October*: Begins writing *Transparent Things*.
1970	*September*: English version of *Mary* published.
1971	*March*: Publication of *Poems and Problems*.
	December: Publication of *Glory*, the last of Nabokov's novels to be translated into English.
1972	*September–October*: Prepares *Strong Opinions* (published 1973).
	October: Publication of *Transparent Things*.
1973	*February*: Begins *Look at the Harlequins!*
	September: Final rift with first biographer, Andrew Field.
1974	*February*: *Lolita: A Screenplay* published.
	May: Plans the writing of a new novel, *The Original of Laura* (never completed).
	August: *Look at the Harlequins!* published.
1976	*March*: *Details of a Sunset and other Stories* published, completing Nabokov's plans for collections of stories.
1977	*2 July*: Dies in hospital in Lausanne.
	7 July: Cremated in Vevey. Buried at Clarens Cemetery.

Bibliography

WORKS BY NABOKOV

Novels and Short Stories

Mary [1926], trans. from the Russian by Michael Glenny with the author (New York: Vintage International, 1989; Harmondsworth: Penguin, 1973).

King, Queen, Knave [1928], trans. from the Russian by Dmitri Nabokov with the author (New York: Vintage International, 1989; Harmondsworth: Penguin, 1993).

The Defense [1929–30], trans. from the Russian by Michael Scammell with the author (New York: Vintage International, 1990); repr. as *The Luzhin Defense* (Harmondsworth: Penguin, 1994).

The Eye [1930], trans. from the Russian by Dmitri Nabokov with the author (New York: Vintage International, 1990; Harmondsworth: Penguin, 1992).

Glory [1931–2], trans. from the Russian by Dmitri Nabokov with the author (New York: Vintage International, 1991; Harmondsworth: Penguin, 1974).

Laughter in the Dark [1932–3], trans. from the Russian by the author (New York: Vintage International, 1989; Harmondsworth: Penguin, 1963).

Despair [1934], trans. from the Russian by the author (London: John Long, 1937); rev. ed., New York: Vintage International, 1989; Harmondsworth: Penguin, 1981).

Invitation to a Beheading (1935–6), trans. from the Russian by Dmitri Nabokov with the author (New York: Vintage International, 1989; Harmondsworth: Penguin, 1963).

The Gift [1937–8], trans. from the Russian by Dmitri Nabokov and Michael Scammell with the author (New York: Vintage International, 1991; Harmondsworth: Penguin, 1981).

The Real Life of Sebastian Knight [1941] (Vintage International, 1992; Harmondsworth: Penguin, 1964).

Bend Sinister [1947] (New York: Vintage International, 1990; Harmondsworth: Penguin, 1974).

Lolita [1955] (New York: Vintage International, 1989; Harmondsworth, Penguin, 1980).

The Annotated Lolita, ed. by Alfred J. Appel, Jr (New York: Vintage International, 1991; Harmondsworth: Penguin, 1995).

Pnin [1957] (New York: Vintage International, 1989; Harmondsworth: Penguin, 1960).

Pale Fire [1962] (New York: Vintage International, 1989; Harmondsworth: Penguin, 1973).

Ada or Ardor: A Family Chronicle [1974] (New York: Vintage International, 1990; Harmondsworth: Penguin, 1970).

Transparent Things [1972] (New York: Vintage International, 1989; Harmondsworth: Penguin, 1975).

Look at the Harlequins! [1974] (New York: Vintage International, 1990; Harmondsworth: Penguin, 1980).

The Enchanter [1939], trans. from the Russian by Dmitri Nabokov (New York: Vintage International, 1991; London: Picador, 1987).

The shorter fiction is complete in *The Stories of Vladimir Nabokov* (New York: Vintage International, 1997); repr. as *Collected Stories* (Harmondsworth: Penguin, 1997).

Poetry and Chess Problems

Poems and Problems (39 Russian Poems, 14 English Poems, 18 Chess Problems), with English translations by the author (New York: McGraw-Hill, 1970; London: Weidenfeld & Nicolson, 1972).

Drama

The Waltz Invention [1938], trans. from the Russian by Dmitri Nabokov with the author (New York: Phaedra, 1966).

The Man from the USSR and Other Plays, trans. from the Russian and ed. by Dmitri Nabokov (New York: Harcourt Brace Jovanovich/Bruccoli Clark, 1984).

Memoirs, Interviews, Letters and Lepidoptery

Conclusive Evidence: A Memoir (New York: Harper, 1951); repr. as *Speak, Memory: A Memoir* (London: Gollancz, 1951); rev. ed., *Speak, Memory: An Autobiography Revisited* [1967] (New York: Vintage International, 1989; Harmondsworth: Penguin, 1991).

Strong Opinions [1973] (New York: Vintage International, 1990; London: Weidenfeld & Nicolson, 1974).

The Nabokov–Wilson Letters 1940–1977, ed. by Simon Karlinsky (New York: Harper & Row, 1979); rev. and expanded ed. as *Dear Bunny, Dear Volodya* (Berkeley, CA: University of California, 2001).

Vladimir Nabokov: Perepiska s sestroi, ed. by Helene Sikorski (Ann Arbor, MI: Ardis, 1985).

Selected Letters 1940–1977, ed. by Dmitri Nabokov and Matthew J. Bruccoli (New York: Harcourt Brace Jovanovich/Bruccoli Clark Layman, 1989; London: Weidenfeld & Nicolson, 1990).

Nabokov's Butterflies: Unpublished and Uncollected Writings, ed. by Brian Boyd and Robert Michael Pyle (Harmondsworth: Allen Lane, The Penguin Press, 2000).

Literary Criticism

Nikolai Gogol (Norfolk, CT: New Directions, 1944; Oxford: Oxford University Press, 1985).

Lectures on Literature, ed. by Fredson Bowers (New York: Harcourt Brace Jovanovich, 1980: London: Picador, 1983).

Lectures on Russian Literature, ed. by Fredson Bowers (New York: Harcourt Brace Jovanovich, 1981; London: Picador, 1983).

Translations

A Hero of Our Time by Mikhail Lermontov, trans. by Vladimir Nabokov in collaboration with Dmitri Nabokov (New York: Doubleday, 1958; Oxford: Oxford University Press, 1984).

The Song of Igor's Campaign: An Epic of the Twelfth Century [Anonymous], trans. by Vladimir Nabokov (New York: Vintage, 1960; London: Weidenfeld & Nicolson, 1961).

Eugene Onegin: A Novel in Verse by Aleksandr Pushkin, Bollingen Series 72, trans. with commentary by Vladimir Nabokov, 4 vols. (New York: Bollingen; London: Routledge, 1964; rev. ed., Princeton, NJ: Princeton University Press, 1975).

SECONDARY READING

Alexandrov, Vladimir E., ed., *The Garland Companion to Vladimir Nabokov* (New York and London: Garland, 1995).

Appel, Alfred J., Jr, *Nabokov's Dark Cinema* (New York: Oxford University Press, 1974).

Berberova, Nina, *The Italics are Mine: An Autobiography*, trans. by Philippe Radley (New York: Harcourt Brace and World, 1969; repr., New York: Knopf, 1992), Part Four: 'The Salt of the Earth'.

Boyd, Brian, *Vladimir Nabokov: The Russian Years* (Princeton, NJ: Princeton University Press, 1990; London: Chatto & Windus, 1990).

———, *Vladimir Nabokov: The American Years* (Princeton, NJ: Princeton University Press, 1991; London: Chatto & Windus, 1992).

Field, Andrew, *Nabokov: His Life in Art* (Boston: Little, Brown; London: Hodder & Stoughton, 1967).

———, *Nabokov: His Life in Part* (New York: Viking; London: Hamish Hamilton, 1977).

Figes, Orlando, *A People's Tragedy: The Russian Revolution 1891–1924* (London: Pimlico, 1996).

Johnson, Kurt and Steve Coates, *Nabokov's Blues: The Scientific Odyssey of a Literary Genius* (Cambridge, MA: Zoland, 1999).

Schiff, Stacy, *Véra (Mrs Vladimir Nabokov)* (New York: Random House; London: Macmillan, 1999).

Wilson, Edmund, *A Window on Russia: For the Use of Foreign Readers* (New York: Farrar, Straus & Giroux, 1972).

Web Site

ZEMBLA: The Web Site for Vladimir Nabokov, URL: http://www.libraries.psu.edu/iasweb/nabokov/nsintro.htm

List of Illustrations

Every effort has been made to contact all copyright holders. The publishers will be happy to make good in future editions any errors or omissions brought to their attention.

Page

ii Nabokov, Paris, 1939. (Courtesy of the Vladimir Nabokov Estate)

3 (left) Front cover of *Kamera obskura* (Paris and Berlin: Sovremennye zapiski and Parabola, 1933). (Photo: Michael Juliar)

3 (right) Dust jacket of *Laughter in the Dark* (Indianapolis and New York: Bobbs-Merrill, 1938). (Photo: Michael Juliar)

5 Dust jacket of *King, Queen, Knave*, first American paperback edition (Greenwich, CT: Fawcett Crest, 1969). (Courtesy of Juan Martinez/www.fulmerford.com)

7 Photo of Nabokov in 1929 at work on *The Defense*. (Courtesy of the Vladimir Nabokov Estate)

8 Nabokov composing *Lolita* on the road in the late 1940s and early 1950s: a reconstruction for *Life Magazine*, 1958. (Photo © Carl Mydans/Timepix/Rex Features)

9 Nabokov writing at his lectern, Montreux, 1966. (Courtesy of the Vladimir Nabokov Estate)

10 Monument to Colonel Nikolai M. Przhevalsky in the Aleksandrovsky (now Admiralty) Gardens, St Petersburg. (Photo: Jane Grayson)

11 Ex libris Vladimir Dmitrievich Nabokov. (Courtesy of the Vladimir Nabokov Museum, St Petersburg)

12 The Nabokov's town house, 47 Bolshaya Morskaya: photo of the gateway. (Courtesy of Dmitri Nabokov, Montreux)

13 Photograph of Nevsky prospekt in the early 1900s.

14–15 Map of St Petersburg inner town showing: the Nabokov town house; the Tenishev School; and the Tauride Palace.

16 (above, a) Photo of Nabokov's father's father. (Courtesy of the Vladimir Nabokov Estate)

16 (above, b) Nabokov's father's mother. (Courtesy of the Vladimir Nabokov Estate)

16 (above, c) Nabokov's mother's father. (Courtesy of the Vladimir Nabokov Museum, St Petersburg)

40 (**above**) Tsar Nicholas and the Tsarevich Aleksey, with his four daughters and officers of the Cossack escort during the First World War.

40 (**below**) Photograph of schoolmaster and his pupils, Rozhdestveno, 1914. (Courtesy of Vladimir Nabokov Museum at Rozhdestveno)

42 (**above**) Postcard with photograph of red Opel Torpedo 1911. (Author collection)

42 (**below**) Photograph of Yuri Rausch von Traubenberg in uniform. (Courtesy of Dmitri Nabokov, Montreux)

43 (**above**) Photograph of the five Romanov children, *c.* 1910. (Photo: David King Collection)

43 (**below**) Photograph of the five Nabokov children in Yalta, November 1918. (Courtesy of the Vladimir Nabokov Estate)

44 Chess problem composed by Nabokov, from his Crimea notebook (1919). (Courtesy of the Berg Collection, New York Public Library)

46 The Sirin bird. A watercolour Russian *lubok*. (Courtesy of the State Historical Museum, Moscow)

47 Nabokov as an undergraduate at Trinity College, Cambridge, November 1919. (Courtesy of the Vladimir Nabokov Estate)

48 Nabokov on a rowing boat on the Cam, 1920. (Courtesy of the Vladimir Nabokov Estate)

49 Title-page of Nabokov's notebook entitled 'Nostalgia: Stikhi' (April 1920–July 1921). (Courtesy of the Berg Collection, New York Public Library)

51 The poet Rupert Brooke. (Reproduced by permission of King's College Library, Cambridge)

52 Portrait of Aleksandr Blok by Somov (1907). (Photo: David King Collection)

53 (**left**) Sketch made by Pushkin of his friend the poet Kondratii Ryleev, 1826.

53 (**right**) Sketches by Pushkin of hanged men drawn in manuscript margins in 1820s.

54 Edition of *Rul'*, Thursday 30 March 1922, announcing the death of Nabokov's father. (Photo © British Library Newspaper Library, Colindale)

56 Nabokov with his fiancée Svetlana Siewert, Berlin, 1922. (Courtesy of the Vladimir Nabokov Estate)

57 Elena Ivanova Nabokov, 1931. (Courtesy of the Vladimir Nabokov Estate)

58 Véra Evseevna Slonim in Berlin, mid-1920s. (Courtesy of the Vladimir Nabokov Estate)

59 Véra Slonim and Vladimir Nabokov, Berlin, 1923. (Courtesy of the Vladimir Nabokov Estate)

61 (**above**) Nabokov's advertisement in *Rul'*, 2 February 1927. (Photo © British Library Newspaper Library, Colindale)

90 (**below**) Photograph of butterfly, *Neonympha dorothea*, by Jeff Mermelstein. (American Museum of Natural History)

92 Photograph by Constantin Joffé of Nabokov at work in Museum of Comparative Zoology, Harvard. (Courtesy of *Vogue*. Copyright © 1947 (renewed 1975) by the Condé Nast Publication, Inc.)

94 (**left**) Photograph of Edmund Wilson and Mary McCarthy, 1941–2, by Sylvia Salmi. (Courtesy Special Collections, Vasser College Library)

94 (**right**) Drawing of a butterfly by Nabokov, 3 January 1944. (Courtesy of the Vladimir Nabokov Estate)

95 John Updike in 1960, aged twenty-eight. (Photo: Corbis/Bettman)

97 First page of the manuscript of *Conclusive Evidence* (1951). (Courtesy of Dmitri Nabokov, Montreux)

98 (**above**) Nabokov's index-card notes used in preparing *Lolita*. (Courtesy of Dmitri Nabokov, Montreux)

98 (**below**) Viyella advertisement. (Photo: Advertising Archives, London)

100 (**above**) First edition of *Lolita* (Paris: Olympia Press, 1955). (Courtesy Glenn Horowitz Booksellers, New York)

100 (**below**) Cover of the first edition of *Pnin* (Garden City New York: Doubleday, 1957). (Photo: Michael Juliar)

101 The Mondadori reception for *Lolita*, Milan, December 1959. (Photo © Federico Patellani, courtesy of Dmitri Nabokov, Montreux)

102 The Nabokovs at Highland Road, Cayuga Heights, Ithaca, New York, 1957. (Division of Rare & Manuscript Collections, Cornell University Library)

103 Still of Sue Lyon from Stanley Kubrick's *Lolita* (Metro Goldwyn Mayer, 1962). (Photo: Kobal Collection, London)

104 (**above, left**) Photograph of Dmitri rock climbing. (Courtesy of Dmitri Nabokov Montreux)

104 (**above, right**) Track-team, Harvard, 1951–2. (Courtesy of Dmitri Nabokov, Montreux)

104 (**below, left**) Photograph of Dmitri in his Triumph sports car. (Courtesy of Dmitri Nabokov, Montreux)

104 (**below, right**) Photograph of Dmitri in US army uniform. (Courtesy of Dmitri Nabokov, Montreux)

107 Photograph of Nabokov in the garden of the Montreux Palace Hotel. (Photo © Henry Grossman)

108 Photograph of Elena Sikorski (Nabokov's sister) with her son, Vladimir, Prague, 1940s. (Courtesy of Dmitri Nabokov, Montreux)

109 Nabokov with a copy of *Russkaya mysl* (*Russian Thought*), Montreux. (Photo © Jochen Richter/Bayerische Fernsehen)

111 First men on the moon, 20 July 1969. (Photo: Corbis)